# BUSINESS BELIEFS

A COMPANION WORKBOOK

HOLLY WORTON

# CONTENTS

A CIP catalogue record for this book is available from the British Library



First edition: 2016
Second edition: 2020

Published by Tribal Publishing Ltd

# INTRODUCTION TO THE WORKBOOK

I truly hope that you enjoyed my book *Business Beliefs: Upgrade Your Mindset to Overcome Self Sabotage, Achieve Your Goals, and Transform Your Business (and Life).* When I wrote the book, it was not meant to be a motivational self help book; it was meant to be a very experiential book.

In the interest of making it as easy as possible for you to take action on the topics I explored in *Business Beliefs*, I've created this workbook. It contains the fifteen categories of business beliefs, question to help you delve deeper so you can get clear on your current mindset and the mindset you want to have, and a list of journal prompts. Most importantly, it's got space for you to make your own notes and record your own observations about your experiences.

As a reminder, I've also created a little online space with a guided meditations and other materials that will help you to work through some of these activities. You can access these free resources by going to http://hollyworton.com/bbb.

I hope you find this workbook to be useful!

1

# HOW TO USE THIS WORKBOOK

How you use this workbook is entirely up to you, and you alone will know the best way for you to work through the chapters based on what's right for *you*. You're the one who is actually going to do the work here. Be sure to tailor this to fit your own personal wants and needs.

You can use this workbook in a variety of ways:

- Read each chapter in order: do the work and answer the journal prompts that correspond to each chapter
- Dip in and out as you like
- Open the book at a random point and work on the chapter that you open up to
- Read through the table of contents and pick whichever chapter stands out to you

I do, however, suggest that you work on Chapter 2 first. That will help you to get clear on your big business vision so you know exactly what you want to be experiencing in your business and life. Then, the journal prompts in the individual categories will help you to delve even deeper into your mindset around each of the categories as they relate to your big vision.

And if you somehow came across this workbook without having read the original book, *Business Beliefs: Upgrade Your Mindset to Overcome Self Sabotage, Achieve Your Goals, and Transform Your Business (and Life)*, I'd recommend that you stop right now and get that book. It's available in ebook, paperback, and audiobook formats, and it's got vital information that will provide the foundation for the work you do in this workbook. This workbook is intended to support the original book and help you to go deeper. It's not intended as a stand-alone book.

Are you ready? Let's get started.

2

# GET CLEAR ON WHAT YOU WANT

Before we get into the different categories of beliefs and the belief statements themselves, it's important for you to know what you want. Are you 100% clear on the vision you have for your business and life? How do you want to step into your greatness and become a leader in your field? What do you want to experience in your business and life?

I've got a guided meditation that can help you relax and feel into your ideal day and your vision of what you want for your business and life. You can get that at www.hollyworton.com/bbb. If you're not a fan of guided meditations, that's fine. Just answer the questions below on your own.

## Visual

Let's imagine that you've fully stepped into your greatness and that you're living your big vision for your business and life.

* * *

What does stepping into your greatness mean to you?

________________________________________
________________________________________
________________________________________
________________________________________
________________________________________
________________________________________
________________________________________
________________________________________
________________________________________
________________________________________

What does that look like?

What do you see yourself doing?

How do you see yourself starting your day? What time do you get up? Do you set an alarm, or do you wake up naturally?

What does your morning ritual look like? How long does it last?

What do you eat/drink in the morning?

What do you do once your morning routine is over?

What time do you start working?

Do you work from home, or do you leave home to work?

What does your office or work space look like?

What do you work on? Your own creative projects? Do you do work for clients or with clients?

If you're working with clients, what does this look like?
Envision yourself with one of these ideal clients.

Are you writing, creating art, or content for your business? Envision yourself doing whatever it is that you'll be doing once you've achieved this goal of your ideal business.

Take a look at your bank account. Either look at your bank statement, or access your account on your computer. Now that you've got your ideal business, how much money is in your checking/current account? And how much do you have in savings? How much do you have in investments and in your pension/retirement fund?

What does the rest of your day look like?

What do you eat/drink throughout the day?

What else do you do throughout the afternoon?

What time do you wrap up your work or creative activities?

What does your lifestyle look like? What else are you doing in your life, when you're not working directly on your business? What do you see yourself doing?

What do you see yourself doing for exercise/fitness?

What time of the day do you exercise?

Where do you see yourself living? What country are you in? What city, town, or village? Is it an urban environment, or is it rural?

What does your home look like?

What does your evening or nighttime routine look like?

How long does it last?

Is there anything else you need to look at so that you have a clear vision of what your life looks like now that you've fully stepped into your greatness and are living the life of your dreams? Take a few seconds to look at that.

As you reflect on your day, you see how your ideal day is different from your current lifestyle. What are some other things that are different?

## Auditory

Once you've fully stepped into your greatness, what will you be saying to yourself? It could be: "I'm proud of myself," "I can't believe I did this," "I'm so happy that I made it," etc.

What will you hear other people saying about you? It could be: "She's amazing", "Wow, I can't believe what she's done with her business", or something else.

What are your clients saying about you?

What else do you hear in your life, now that you've fully stepped into your greatness? What's going on in the background as you live your day? Do you hear children? Pets? Birds? Music? Other people?

Is your home in a quiet area, or is it bustling and active? What about your office or workplace?

## Kinesthetic

How do you feel when you wake up in the morning?

How do you feel throughout the day? What are your energy levels like? What emotions are you feeling?

How do you feel in the evening as you're getting ready for bed?

Now that you've fully stepped into your greatness . . . how do you feel? Are you feeling free? Satisfied? Proud of yourself? Excited about the future? Write down *all the things* you feel.

What do you feel grateful for about your ideal lifestyle?

## Dial it up

Oftentimes, our vision for ourselves is limited by our beliefs. Read through your answers and mark any details where you're playing small or hesitating to really dream big. Dial up the intensity and the bigness of your vision: How can you make it better, more exciting, or more satisfying? No one else has to see this but you, so don't be afraid to make your dream bigger, better, and bolder. Make notes alongside your original responses in a different color so you can see this new level of your vision. As you dial up the intensity of this vision, pay attention to any fears or limiting beliefs that you have, and write those down.

What fears do you have about living this ideal lifestyle?

What will people think of you?

Will you lose family or friends with this lifestyle change?

What will they say about you?

Do you believe you're worthy of having this dream?

Are you deserving of living this life of your dreams?

Think about all the "what ifs" and "yes, buts"—all the excuses that might get in the way of you working to achieve your dream. Write down all these excuses so you can get them out of your head and onto paper so you can work on them.

## Repeat

You can repeat this visualization or this process as many times as you like. You may want to repeat it on a quarterly basis, so you can get clarity on how your vision has grown and changed over the previous months. As we grow, our vision for our business changes, and it's important for us to understand exactly how our ideal business vision changes over time so we can adjust our goals, strategy and business plan accordingly.

When we're not in a good place, it can be hard to really tap into our greatness and see what it is. So give yourself permission to dream big and to repeat this process regularly, so you can gradually step up your vision of what you want for your business and your life. Each time, you'll expand your vision of what's possible for your business and life. Use a different colored pen each time so you can see how your vision gets gradually upgraded.

## Action plan

What are the top three actions you could take this week to bring you closer to stepping into your vision for your ideal business and lifestyle? Write them down here, along with the dates and times that you'll commit to doing them. Make sure you have the time in your calendar to complete these actions. If the coming week is unusually busy, allow yourself extra time to complete them.

1.

2.

3.

## Business beliefs

Looking at your list of top three actions, answer the following question: who do you need to be to take these actions?

What do you need to believe about yourself to allow you to easily take these actions?

What might stop you from taking these actions?

What would you rather have instead of these blocks that might prevent you from taking action?

How would you rather feel about your action plan?

What do you need to do/experience instead?

What do you need to believe about yourself and your ability to complete this action plan?

Who do you need to be to fully step into your greatness and to achieve your big business vision?

What's stopping you from stepping into your greatness?

## Wrap it up

Is there anything else you need to add to the vision?

Are there any specific goals that you need to add that you want to achieve as part of your vision for stepping into your greatness?

Get it all out and into words that you can see. That will make it easier for you to identify specific beliefs in the lists that follow.

3

# CATEGORIES OF BELIEFS

I've divided up these belief statements into fifteen categories, which I consider to be the most important facets of business mindset that I've regularly worked on with clients over the years. You may find that you have more work to do in some areas, and you may find that you have very little work to do in other areas. In any case, it's worth muscle testing your beliefs to see what the highest priorities are to work on, as your higher self will know what your conscious mind may not be aware of. Remember, depending on what type of work you do to transform your business beliefs, you may want to choose specific beliefs to program into your subconscious, or you might use some of the beliefs as part of a larger intention or goal.

If you previously downloaded the first edition of this book, you may remember that there were over six hundred belief statements included. Now there are more than one thousand. I was very pleased to go through my old journals from the last couple of years and discover hundreds of belief statements that I had created and worked on programming into my subconscious.

The most fascinating part of reviewing my journal and selecting specific belief statements to add to this book was that I was able to see how big I was thinking last year when I was doing this work, and also how many of the things that I worked on have come to pass. It was a very clear reminder of how powerful this work is, and that when we transform beliefs at the deeper levels, it makes it much, much easier for us to achieve our goals. Which leads me to the first category . . .

## Action and Goals

What beliefs do you have about yourself and your ability to take action?

Are you an action taker? Are you a go-getter?

Are you good at getting things done? Or are you "lazy"?

Are you a procrastinator? What do you do when you procrastinate? What types of activities do you procrastinate on?

Think about what types of actions you need to take to step into your greatness and achieve your big vision for your business and life. What do you need to do differently?

Think about what specific goals you need to set. Write them down here.

What are you currently procrastinating on in your business that you would like to take action on?

What new or different actions would you like to take in order to achieve your business goals?

Think about the new or different actions you need to take so you can step into your greatness and achieve your big vision for your business and life. What else do you need/ want to do?

How will you know when you've achieved your current goals and taken the actions you want to take? What will you see/do/feel/hear that will be your confirmation that you've taken these actions?

What do you need to *do* to make this happen?

Who do you need to *be* to make this happen?

What do you need to *believe* about yourself and your ability to achieve these goals and take these actions?

What might stop you from making this happen?

Can you think of any advantage to maintaining your current situation? Are there any benefits for things to stay the way they are and not change?

What fears and limiting beliefs come up for you as you think about taking these actions? Write them all down here.

## Change and Growth

What are you currently experiencing in your business that you would like to change?

How would you like your life/business to be different? What do you want it to be like? Look like? Feel like?

Think about how you need to change so you can step into your greatness and achieve your big vision for your business and life. What else needs to change?

How will you know when you've achieved your current goals and made the changes you want? What will you see/do/feel/hear that will be your confirmation that you've made these changes?

What do you need to *do* to make this happen?

Who do you need to *be* to make this happen?

What do you need to *believe* about yourself and your ability to achieve this goal?

What might stop you from making this happen?

Can you think of any advantage to maintaining your current situation? Are there any benefits for things to stay the way they are and not change?

In what other ways do you need or want to grow as a business owner or entrepreneur? How do you feel about growth? Does it feel stressful? Does it make you anxious?

Are you afraid of change, or do you embrace it?

Are you a risk taker? On a scale of 1 to 10—with 10 being highest—how comfortable are you with taking risks in your business and life?

What other fears and limiting beliefs come up for you as you think about growth and change? Write everything down here.

## Clients

What are you currently experiencing with your clients that you would like to change?

Are you experiencing any boundary issues with clients that you would like to change?

What new boundaries do you need to implement—and uphold—in your business?

What would you do in a situation where a client is late or doesn't show up at all? How long would you wait? Will the client forfeit what they've paid, or will you transfer their payment to another date and time?

How would you like your work with your clients to be different? What do you want it to be like? Look like? Feel like?

How do you want to attract a steady stream of your ideal clients into your business?

What do you need to do to attract a steady stream of ideal clients?

What you need to do to have a thriving business with a calendar full of ideal clients . . . and maybe even a waiting list?

What do you believe about your ability to create your ideal workload of clients?

How will you know when you've achieved your current goals and made the changes you want in terms of your work with clients? What will you see/do/feel/hear that will be your confirmation that you've made these changes?

What do you need to *do* to make this happen?

Who do you need to *be* to make this happen?

What do you need to *believe* about yourself and your ability to achieve this goal?

What might stop you from making this happen?

Can you think of any advantage to maintaining your current situation? Are there any benefits for things to stay the way they are and not change?

What other fears and limiting beliefs come up for you as you think about clients and boundaries? Write everything down here.

## Confidence and Self Trust

How confident do you currently feel? How much do you trust yourself on a scale of 1 to 10, with 10 being highest?

How would you like this to be different? How would your business be different if you were confident in yourself and trusted yourself completely? What would that look like? Feel like?

Do you want to be more confident in yourself and your abilities? Do you want to be more sure of yourself when speaking and writing? In expressing yourself and your message online? Where else do you want more confidence in your business?

How will you know when you're feeling more confident and trusting yourself more? What will you see/do/feel/hear that will be your confirmation that you've made these changes?

What do you need to *do* to make this happen?

Who do you need to *be* to make this happen?

What do you need to *believe* about yourself and your ability to achieve this goal?

What might stop you from making this happen?

Can you think of any advantage to maintaining your current levels of confidence and lack of self-trust? Are there any benefits for things to stay the way they are and not change?

What other fears and limiting beliefs come up for you as you think about confidence and self-trust? Write everything down here.

## Creativity

What are you currently experiencing in your business in terms of creativity that you would like to change?

How would you like to express yourself creatively in your business? What would it look like for you to fully express your creativity? What would that feel like?

How will you know when you've achieved your current creative goals and made the changes you want? What will you see/do/feel/hear that will be your confirmation that you've made these changes?

What do you need to *do* to make this happen?

Who do you need to *be* to make this happen?
What do you need to *believe* about yourself and your ability to achieve this goal?

What do you need to believe about your ability to write blog posts? About your ability to write a book? To record inspiring videos? To create a podcast that gets tens of thousands of downloads?

What do you need to believe about your ability to be more creative in your business?

What might stop you from making this happen?

Can you think of any advantage to maintaining your current situation? Are there any benefits for things to stay the way they are and not change?

What other fears and limiting beliefs come up for you as you think about your ability to be a creative entrepreneur? Write everything down here.

## Leadership and Outsourcing

Do you see yourself as a leader? Why or why not?

Do you want to be seen as a thought leader? Do you feel strong and grounded enough to step up as a thought leader and speak your truth?

Do you feel ready to inspire people on a greater scale? How would that make you feel to be an inspiration to others?

How else would you like to step up as a leader? What do you want to be doing? What would that look like? Feel like?

What do you need to *do* to make this happen?

Who do you need to *be* to make this happen?

What do you need to *believe* about yourself and your ability to achieve this goal?

What might stop you from making this happen?

Can you think of any advantage to maintaining your current situation? Are there any benefits for things to stay the way they are and not change?

Think about what you need to believe about your ability to outsource tasks that aren't within your zone of genius. Are you ready, willing, and able to hire and manage people as part of your business team—either as full-time staff or freelancers?

What other fears and limiting beliefs come up for you as you think about leadership and outsourcing? Write everything down here.

## Learning

Is learning easy for you?

Are you easily able to teach yourself all the things you know about running an online business?

When you meet an obstacle, can you quickly do an online search and find the solution? Or do you stay stuck where you are?

What do you need to believe about yourself in order for learning to be easier?

Would you like to change how you feel about your ability to learn new things? How would you like to feel about your ability to learn new things?

What do you need to *do* to make this happen?

Who do you need to *be* to make this happen?

What do you need to *believe* about yourself and your ability to achieve this goal?

What might stop you from making this happen?

Can you think of any advantage to maintaining your current situation? Are there any benefits for things to stay the way they are and not change?

What other fears and limiting beliefs come up for you as you think about learning? Write everything down here.

## Lifestyle

What are you currently experiencing in your life that you would like to change?

How would you like your lifestyle to be different? What do you want it to be like? Look like? Feel like?

What does your ideal lifestyle look like?

How does your business fit into this ideal lifestyle? Be sure you plan your business accordingly. If you want plenty of freedom and space to do what you want, you may want to focus more on passive income than on one-to-one client services. Group services are kind of a happy medium between the two.

How will you know when you've achieved your current goals and achieved the lifestyle that you want? What will you see/do/feel/hear that will be your confirmation that you've made these changes?

What do you need to *do* to make this happen?

Who do you need to *be* to make this happen?

What do you need to *believe* about yourself and your ability to achieve this goal?

What might stop you from making this happen?

Can you think of any advantage to maintaining your current situation? Are there any benefits for things to stay the way they are and not change?

What other fears and limiting beliefs come up for you as you think about changing your lifestyle? Write everything down here.

## Marketing and Sales

What does your current marketing and sales plan look, and how would you like to change that?

What do you want your marketing and sales efforts to be like? Look like? Feel like?

What beliefs do you have about your ability to market your business, both online and offline?

What beliefs do you have about your ability to have effective sales conversations with potential clients?

How will you know when you've achieved your current goals and made the changes you want? What will you see/do/feel/hear that will be your confirmation that you've made these changes?

What do you need to *do* to make this happen?

Who do you need to *be* to make this happen?

What do you need to *believe* about yourself and your ability to achieve this goal?

What might stop you from making this happen?

Can you think of any advantage to maintaining your current situation? Are there any benefits for things to stay the way they are and not change?

What other fears and limiting beliefs come up for you as you think about marketing and sales? Write everything down here.

## Money

What's your current turnover in your business? What are your profits?

How would you like your business and personal income to be different?

How would you like to change how you save and investment money?

Would you like to hire (new) advisors to help you with your investments? How would you like them to be different from your current advisors, assuming you have them?

How will you know when you've achieved your current money goals and made the changes you want? What will you see/do/feel/hear that will be your confirmation that you've made these changes?

What do you need to *do* to make this happen?

Who do you need to *be* to make this happen?

What do you need to *believe* about yourself and your ability to achieve this goal?

What might stop you from making this happen?

Can you think of any advantage to maintaining your current money situation? Are there any benefits for things to stay the way they are and not change?

What other fears and limiting beliefs come up for you as you think about money? Write everything down here.

## Personal Power

How do you currently feel about your sense of personal power, and how would you would like to change that?

How powerful do you feel on a scale of 1 to 10, with 10 being highest?

How do you feel about the word "power"? Do you see it as good, bad, or neutral?

How would you like your sense of personal power to be different? What do you want it to be like? Look like? Feel like?

How will you know when you've achieved your current goals and made the changes you want? What will you see/do/feel/hear that will be your confirmation that you've made these changes?

What do you need to *do* to make this happen?

Who do you need to *be* to make this happen?

What do you need to *believe* about yourself and your ability to achieve this goal?

What might stop you from making this happen?

Can you think of any advantage to maintaining your current situation? Are there any benefits for things to stay the way they are and not change?

What other fears and limiting beliefs come up for you as you think about personal power? Write everything down here.

## Strategy, Clarity and Vision

Think back to your big business vision. Reflect on what you want for your business and life. What are you currently experiencing in your business that you would like to change so that it's more aligned with your big business vision?

How will you know when you've achieved your current goals and made the changes you want? What will you see/do/feel/hear that will be your confirmation that you've made these changes?

What do you need to *do* to make this happen?

Who do you need to *be* to make this happen?

What do you need to *believe* about yourself and your ability to achieve this goal?

What might stop you from making this happen?

Can you think of any advantage to maintaining your current situation? Are there any benefits for things to stay the way they are and not change?

What other fears and limiting beliefs come up for you as you think about strategy, clarity, and vision? Write everything down here.

## Success and Opportunities

Think about what opportunities you've ignored or turned down in the past due to fears or limiting beliefs. Were you ever approached for a speaking engagement that you turned down due to fear?

Did anyone ever invite you to be a guest on their podcast or write a guest post for their blog, yet you balked because you were afraid of showing up for a new audience?

Have you ever been approached to do a joint venture with another entrepreneur, but you hesitated and lost the opportunity?

How do you define success?

What would make you feel more successful in your business?

What does success look like to you ? What would it feel like?

How will you know when you're successful? What will you see/do/feel/hear that will be your confirmation that you've "made it"?

What opportunities would you would like to attract into your business? What opportunities you would like to actively pursue?

What do you need to *do* to make this happen?

Who do you need to *be* to make this happen?

What do you need to *believe* about yourself and your ability to achieve this goal?

What might stop you from making this happen?

Can you think of any advantage to maintaining your current situation? Are there any benefits for things to stay the way they are and not change?

How do you think your life will change once you create the successful business of your dreams? How do you think your family and friends will respond? Do you have any fears about losing friendships?

What other fears and limiting beliefs come up for you as you think about success and opportunities? Write everything down here.

## Value and Self-Worth

Do you truly value your knowledge, skills, and experience? Do you value your uniqueness? Do your rates and prices for your products and services reflect this?

How do you currently feel about the value of what you offer? Do you think the prices of your products and services reflect your true value? Do you think that perhaps you overvalue or undervalue them?

How would you like your self-worth to be different? What do you want it to be like? Look like? Feel like?

How will you know when you've achieved your current goals and made the changes you want? What will you see/do/feel/hear that will be your confirmation that you've made these changes?

What do you need to *do* to make this happen?

Who do you need to *be* to make this happen?

What do you need to *believe* about yourself and your ability to achieve this goal?

What might stop you from making this happen?

Can you think of any advantage to maintaining your current situation? Are there any benefits for things to stay the way they are and not change?

What other fears and limiting beliefs come up for you as you think about value and self-worth? Write everything down here.

## Visibility

On a scale of 1 to 10, with 10 being highest, how visible do you think you are with your business?

How well known are you as a leader in your field?

If your business were more visible, what would that look like? What would be different? How would that make you feel?

Think about what types of actions you need to take to show up in the world in a big way with your business. How could you market your products and services in a bigger way?

How could you show up and really *shine* as an entrepreneur?

Make a list of at least ten well known entrepreneurs that you admire. What things do they do that make them stand out? How do they do things differently? What can you do to be more like them?

And when you think about doing these things, what fears pop up for you? What beliefs come up? Do you think: "Yes, but she's thinner/prettier/smarter/whatever"? What are the "yes, buts" that come up for you? Write it all down here.

How will you know when you've achieved your current goals and made the changes you want? What will you see/do/feel/hear that will be your confirmation that you've made these changes?

What do you need to *do* to make this happen?

Who do you need to *be* to make this happen?

What do you need to *believe* about yourself and your ability to achieve this goal?

What might stop you from making this happen?

Can you think of any advantage to maintaining your current situation? Are there any benefits for things to stay the way they are and not change?

What other fears and limiting beliefs come up for you as you think about visibility? Write everything down here.

4

# ACTION AND GOALS

1. I easily achieve my business goals.

2. I have the drive to conquer obstacles and achieve my goals.

3. I have the self discipline to focus on my most important tasks each day.

4. I am extremely motivated and focused in working on my business.

5. It's easy for me to focus on high-priority tasks to help my business grow.

6. I am disciplined and goal oriented.

7. I always feel motivated to get things done in my business.

8. I transform my reality to align with my goals.

9. I am focused, driven, and decisive.

10. I get things done quickly and easily and with plenty of time to relax.

11. I am clear, organized, and focused.

12. I am inspired to take action, and I do!

13. It's easy for me to take action to make my business a reality.

14. I am organized and consistent in my project management.

15. It's easy and effortless for me to identify my top priorities and take action on them.

16. I am organized with my time and I follow through with things.

17. I trust myself to take the necessary action to create a successful business.

18. I easily develop my great ideas through action.

19. I have the drive and energy to take action in my business.

20. It's safe and appropriate for me to take action and move forward.

21. I act calmly and decisively and with clear focus.

22. I set clear and specific goals and I take action toward achieving them.

23. I take consistent, inspired action in my business.

24. My actions are rooted in my clear vision for my business.

25. I easily create with focus and divine inspiration.

26. I'm so excited to launch [name of product or service] to the world.

27. I take action when inspiration comes to me.

28. Taking action builds my confidence and courage.

29. I live in the flow of my life purpose, and my actions are easy to take.

30. It's easy and effortless for me to take action toward my business goals.

31. I easily follow through and complete all my projects.

32. I easily maintain the perfect balance between work and play.

33. All my actions support my goals and dreams.

34. I act on every opportunity that is aligned with my vision.

35. I enjoy taking action and getting things done.

36. I take responsibility for my business by taking inspired action every day.

37. Every inspired action I take creates wonderful new opportunities for me.

38. With each action I take, I become more inspired and motivated.

39. I easily create [name of product, project, or service] now.

40. I'm both efficient with and respectful of time.

41. I work smartly and at lightning speed.

42. I have all the energy I need and more to do the things I want to do.

43. I am super energized into action.

44. Focus is easy for me.

45. I always focus on my highest priority actions.

46. I quickly and easily take action on my ideas.

47. I move forward fearlessly in my life and business.

48. I advance toward my goals deliberately, methodically, and at exactly the right pace.

49. I visualize it and then I do it.

50. It's safe and appropriate for me to listen to and take action on my intuition.

51. I have more than enough time to do all the things I want to do.

52. I relax and take time to respond to difficult messages.

53. I easily take care of all the work needed to make [£€$ amount of money] each month.

54. It's always easy for me to make time to [complete a specific action].

55. Taking action is easy and fun for me.

56. I release stress from my life as I take action with ease.

57. I release stress from my life as I achieve my goals with ease.

58. The more actions I take, the better I feel about myself and my business.

59. I take easy inspired action to achieve my business goals.

60. Inspired action is easy when I listen to my intuition.

61. I take the right actions for me and my business.

62. I release the need for busy work and always focus on high priority actions.

63. I easily focus on the high priority goals in my business.

64. I easily set a goals with appropriate and achievable deadlines.

65. ______________________________

66. ______________________________

67. ______________________________

68. ______________________________

69. ______________________________

70. ______________________________

71. ______________________________

5

# CHANGE AND GROWTH

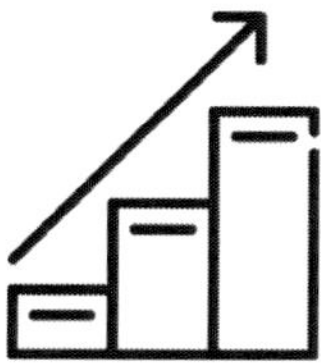

1. Change can be really quick for me.

2. I feel calm, focused, happy, secure and serene when changes are happening.

3. I look forward to change in my life and business.

4. I easily embrace and adapt to change in my business.

5. I welcome changes in my life and business.

6. I am a catalyst for my own change.

7. I am willing to take the necessary risks to change.

8. Change is my friend, as it helps me experience new and exciting things.

9. I enjoy and accept the process of change, including the difficult parts.

10. I actively embrace the opportunities that come with change.

11. I have the power to easily change my business.

12. Change is easy and effortless for me, and I enjoy it.

13. My arms are open to change.

14. It's safe for me to let go of my current business and begin a new one.

15. It's safe and appropriate for my business to change as I do.

16. Change represents freedom and flow and I love it.

17. I have the clarity of vision to see the signs of change and I take action on them.

18. My business evolves and grows as I do.

19. I am agile and I easily change when circumstances call for it.

20. Change helps me learn and grow and I embrace it.

21. I take the necessary risks to change my business when I feel it's time to do so.

22. Change always brings new opportunities and gifts to me.

23. Change helps me grow and evolve as an individual.

24. As I transform myself and my mind, my business transforms.

25. I accept change when it happens.

26. My ability to easily change allows me freedom in life and business.

27. I easily change my business to align it with my values.

28. Change is always positive, as it brings new things to my life and business.

29. My business and I are constantly changing and transforming as we grow.

30. As I change, I feel in flow with my purpose.

31. I love change; it helps me flow with my own personal transformation.

32. My business is expanding and flourishing.

33. It's my time and I'm ready for the next step.

34. My business gives me the perfect opportunities to learn and grow.

35. My business grows easily and effortlessly.

36. I adapt to changes in my life and business easily and effortlessly.

37. I am the most advanced professional version of myself that I can be.

38. It's possible to grow both myself and my business at the same time.

39. I easily rise up to the level of the person I want to be.

40. I am the person I want to be.

41. I easily let go of all that no longer serves me.

42. It's safe and appropriate for me to let go of old friends that I've outgrown.

43. I easily let go of old structures and allow joyful energy to flow through me.

44. I easily release all limitations and allow myself to flourish.

45. I easily break through all limiting boundaries.

46. I blossom like the glorious flower I am.

47. I easily let go of past teachers, mentors, and coaches that I've outgrown.

48. I easily grow and transform my life.

49. I easily reinvent myself.

50. It's easy for me to try on new ways of being.

51. I accept and welcome the changes in my life.

52. I easily trust the process of change and growth.

53. I feel comfortable and excited when going through a transition.

54. My business is growing in accordance with divine timing.

55. Change is easy and fun for me.

56. I release stress from my life as I make changes in my business.

57. Change is stress-free in my business and life.

58. The more inspired changes I make, the better I feel about myself and my business.

59. I take easy inspired action to make changes in my business and life.

60. I take easy inspired action to grow myself and my business.

61. ______________________________

62. ______________________________

63. ______________________________

64. ______________________________

65. ______________________________

66. ______________________________

67. ______________________________

68. ______________________________

69. ______________________________

70. ______________________________

71. ______________________________

72. ______________________________

6

# CLIENTS AND BOUNDARIES

1. I ask all clients for a referral and a testimonial.

2. People are very excited to do business with me!

3. I regularly and consistently attract new clients that I love working with.

4. I give people more than they expect and I am happy to do this.

5. I attract loyal clients to my business who recommend me to others.

6. I have a successful business that improves lives, including mine.

7. It's easy for me to bring in a consistent stream of clients each month.

8. Because I am such a positive resource, people love doing business with me.

9. I am in tune with my clients' needs.

10. I have an excellent business reputation that is backed up with client testimonials.

11. I provide products and services that my target market of clients wants and needs.

12. I have healthy boundaries with my clients.

13. The things I create in business serve to help others.

14. It's easy and effortless for me to attract the right clients for my business.

15. Potential clients trust me because I am trustworthy.

16. I'm capable of helping my ideal clients go from good to great.

17. It's easy and effortless for me to attract clients who are prepared to invest in what I have to offer.

18. I have a steady stream of clients committed to working with me this year.

19. I take responsibility for my relationships with my clients.

20. People recognize that the products and services I create have great benefits.

21. It's easy for me to attract the right people to my business.

22. I have a steady stream of clients who keep coming back for more.

23. My ideal clients easily understand the value of what I have to offer.

24. I attract new paying clients on a daily basis.

25. It's easy for me to communicate my new higher fees to clients.

26. My ideal clients are happy to pay the prices I ask.

27. I attract only uplifting and inspiring clients to my business.

28. When my ideal clients first meet me, they feel instantly drawn to me.

29. My paying clients are 100% happy with the results they get from working with me.

30. It's safe and appropriate for me to take all the time I need to give a quote.

31. It's safe and appropriate for me to channel people to my services and this is easy for me.

32. Boundaries help me create a win-win situation with my clients.

33. I know exactly who my ideal client is and how to communicate with them.

34. It's okay for me to let go of clients who aren't a good fit.

35. I quickly and easily let go of clients when I sense we aren't a good fit.

36. It's easy for me to collect money from clients who need to pay their invoice.

37. It's easy for me to connect with my ideal clients.

38. I have a steady stream of clients who pay for what I love to do.

39. I am booked out with clients for months in advance.

40. I write compelling content that gets me seen online.

41. The more people who know about me, the more people I can help.

42. I attract clients who appreciate me and my work.

43. I have strong boundaries and I communicate them clearly and with love.

44. I have a constant stream of clients who pay me well.

45. I have an easy system for sending contracts to clients.

46. It's easy for me to ask clients to sign contracts.

47. It's easy for me to ask for client referrals.

48. I perfectly manifest a steady stream of clients.

49. I consistently attract clients who see the value in what I have to offer.

50. People pay to hear my message.

51. People want what I have.

52. People are attracted to what I embody.

53. People are longing for what I have to offer.

54. I have the wisdom to know what to change.

55. It's easy for me to find clients who are ready, willing, and able to take action.

56. It's easy for me to fill my calendar with paying clients.

57. Signing up new clients is an easy and streamlined process.

58. I have a client management system that builds great relationships.

59. My ideal clients keep coming back for more.

60. I only attract clients who are a great fit for me.

61. I easily set and uphold boundaries with my clients.

62. I set and uphold clear boundaries regarding client cancellations.

63. I fully value my time and energy, and so do my clients.

64. I attract clients who value my time and work.

65. My clients always reschedule appointments well in advance when they need to.

66. I appreciate and respect my time, and so do my clients.

67. The more I respect my time, the more I encourage my clients to respect their own time.

68. ______________________________

69. ______________________________

7

# CONFIDENCE AND TRUST

1. I am confident and humble.

2. The more confident I am, the more I can be of service to others.

3. There is a way to be both confident and humble and I open myself to the solution now.

4. I am a woman of strength and courage.

5. I am good at business and I have great business sense.

6. I believe in my ability to change the world with the work that I do.

7. I am capable of running my own successful business.

8. I'm confident in what I have to offer clients.

9. I'm confident in my knowledge and experience.

10. I'm confident about asking people to JV with me for business.

11. I let go of all fears of being powerful and successful and replace them with confidence.

12. I am here to fully express myself.

13. I believe in myself, my power, and my abilities.

14. I am confident.

15. I have full trust and belief in myself.

16. I am trustworthy and reliable.

17. I am self-confident and self assured.

18. I can rely on myself and I do.

19. I trust myself to make the business and life decisions that are for my highest good.

20. I feel powerful and confident when speaking.

21. I am sure of myself.

22. It is safe and appropriate for me to be confident and sure of myself.

23. I have courage and I take action accordingly.

24. I am determined to be successful.

25. I trust each and every decision I make.

26. I trust my business to support me.

27. I feel safe, comfortable, and equal in groups.

28. I have faith in myself.

29. I believe in myself and my ability to make a successful business on my terms.

30. I am tenacious.

31. I'm an inspiring and financially successful business woman.

32. I believe in myself and so do other people.

33. I have total faith in myself that I can achieve my business goals.

34. I believe I can make things happen.

35. I am an expert in my field and my ideal clients view me as such.

36. I have all I need to create a successful business.

37. I have the time and energy to create a successful business.

38. I am confident and comfortable with myself.

39. I am quirky and different and I have the confidence to express my differences.

40. I am megaconfident.

41. I easily and confidently express my woo side.

42. I have a well established line of trust with myself.

43. I easily listen to my heart and its wisdom.

44. I believe in myself and my enormous potential.

45. I deeply and completely believe in myself.

46. I trust in my ability to hold space for people.

47. I trust that I can handle myself in case of emergency.

48. I trust I can handle anything that comes my way when I'm holding space for a group.

49. I trust in my ability to create something totally new.

50. I trust in my ability to recognize and receive downloads.

51. I trust I remember all the details from my downloads.

52. I deeply and completely trust myself.

53. I trust in my ability to [insert action of choice].

54. I am safe, confident, and secure in my life.

55. I trust that each step I take is perfectly guided.

56. I trust my inner self.

57. I have invincible confidence in myself.

58. I deeply and completely trust my intuition and always act on it.

59. I confidently position myself as an intuitive business owner.

60. I easily remain connected to my intuition.

61. I release the need for approval and replace it with trust in my own decisions.

62. ______________________________

63. ______________________________

64. ______________________________

65. ______________________________

66. ______________________________

67. ______________________________

68. ______________________________

69. ______________________________

70. ______________________________

71. ______________________________

8

# CREATIVITY

1. My writing is deep and heart-felt.

2. I am highly creative in business and in life.

3. I easily open up and express myself clearly in my creative projects.

4. My mind is open to new creative ideas and inspiration.

5. An endless flow of creativity lies within me.

6. I am always open to creative ideas, thoughts, and perspectives.

7. Expressing my creativity through business gives me great joy.

8. I am a naturally creative person.

9. My business is the perfect way for me to express my creativity.

10. My creativity flows easily and effortlessly.

11. Brilliant business ideas come to me all the time.

12. I am full of inspiration and creativity.

13. Creative energy flows through me every day.

14. I creatively express myself with ease.

15. Creative business ideas come to me regularly.

16. My creative ideas shape how my business grows.

17. With each day I become more creative in business and in life.

18. I am becoming more and more creative with every day.

19. New business ideas flow to me daily.

20. My creative gifts are appreciated by my ideal clients.

21. I allow my creative energy to flow freely at all times.

22. I release all resistance to fully expressing my creativity and I replace it with acceptance.

23. I always pay attention to my creative inspiration.

24. I am a successful writer, and I am extremely creative with words.

25. I am a creative problem solver in business and in life.

26. It's easy and effortless for me to express my creativity through writing.

27. I am a creative visionary in business.

28. My mind is filled with creative ideas.

29. My writing is strengthened by constructive criticism and editing.

30. I express my creativity every day, with confidence and enthusiasm.

31. I deserve the time and space to be creative and inspired.

32. I channel my creativity into successful and profitable projects.

9

## LEADERSHIP AND OUTSOURCING

1. I lead from femininity.

2. I know how to lead in life and business.

3. My ideal clients recognize me as a leader in my field.

4. My tribe trusts my opinions and expertise.

5. It's easy for me to take the lead in business and in life.

6. I am a natural strategic decision maker.

7. I have excellent leadership skills.

8. I regularly seek out new leadership opportunities.

9. I am a born leader and leadership comes easily to me.

10. I embrace responsibility and leadership.

11. I make things happen.

12. I am an inspiring mentor to other entrepreneurs.

13. I inspire others to greatness.

14. I inspire my team to reach their goals.

15. I enjoy working with other people to achieve my business goals.

16. I love being an inspiration to others.

17. My story of personal and professional freedom inspires others to seek the same.

18. My words inspire people all over the world.

19. I inspire others to make a difference in the world.

20. It's easy for me to communicate my vision to my team.

21. I get help when needed to make my business a success.

22. I'm a great entrepreneur and I treat my service providers exceptionally well.

23. I deserve to outsource the things I don't enjoy doing, like housekeeping and admin work.

24. My business can easily support all the staff I need and provide me with free time to enjoy my life.

25. It's safe and appropriate to let my team support me.

26. It's easy to find the perfect freelancers to help me with my business.

27. I have a clear vision of exactly who I need to help me with my business.

28. It's easy for me to find the right person to build process and systems for my business.

29. I'm able to provide a stable work environment for my employees/freelancers.

30. I attract employees/freelancers who are loyal to me and my business.

31. I am an outstanding leader in my field.

32. It's easy for me to create a compelling vision that my team members and I are excited about.

33. I hire people for their strengths and I find ways to support their weaknesses.

34. Collaborating with other entrepreneurs is more fun and profitable than competing with them.

35. I am inspired by the accomplishments of other entrepreneurs.

36. I am fully supported in my vision for my business.

37. It's easy for me to accept help from others.

38. It's safe for me to accept help from other people.

39. It's easy for me to delegate whenever I need to.

40. I can tell who I can trust to delegate to and it's safe to do so.

41. I easily find people who can do things better than me.

42. My greatness shines through my work and my leadership.

43. I trust that I know when and how to delegate tasks.

44. I trust in my ability to manage people so that quality work gets done.

45. I am a thought leader for the change in consciousness.

46. I'm part of the change in consciousness revolution.

47. I have a big role to play and I can do it.

48. Other people are ready, willing, and able to support me.

49. I am known worldwide for [your field of expertise].

50. I am a leader in [your field of expertise].

51. I fully embrace my purpose as a path-maker.

52. I shine my light as a positive authority figure.

53. It's easy for me to ask for and accept help.

54. I'm seen as an expert in my field.

55. I am an expert in my field.

56. It's easy for me to focus on my zone of genius and to outsource the rest.

57. I spend my work days focused on my zone of genius.

58. I have a talented team of people who help me with tasks that are outside my area of expertise.

59. I love building and managing my team of talented people.

60. I'm great at managing the people on my team.

61. ______________________________

62. ______________________________

63. ______________________________

64. ______________________________

65. ______________________________

66. ______________________________

67. ______________________________

68. ______________________________

69. ______________________________

10

# LEARNING

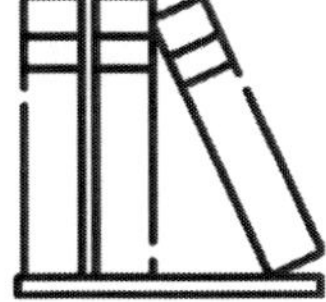

1. Technology comes to me easily and effortlessly.

2. I easily embrace new concepts and ideas.

3. It's easy for me to learn new things.

4. I love learning new things.

5. Any information I need to recall comes effortlessly to mind.

6. I easily learn anything I need to know.

7. Every day I improve my ability to retain information.

8. Each day I learn something new and exciting.

9. I easily absorb new knowledge and concepts.

10. I am able to remember all information when needed with ease and clarity.

11. I am eager to learn new things for my business.

12. I embrace the idea that being an entrepreneur involves learning new things.

13. I am completely at ease when learning new concepts.

14. I am fully committed to learning what I need to learn to make my business a success.

15. I am motivated to learn new things and I am confident in my ability to retain new information.

16. I love learning about business and marketing.

17. I love that owning a business means I get to learn new things.

18. Being an entrepreneur means that I am constantly learning.

19. I have a great business mentor who guides me to learn new things.

20. My business mentor helps me learn what I need to grow my business.

21. Learning is easy when I have a business mentor who is aligned with my values.

22. Learning is fun and exciting!

23. Learning new things opens my mind to new concepts and ideas.

24. It's easy for me to understand what my preferred method of learning is.

25. I clearly see what I need to learn in my business and I take action toward learning it.

26. I am inspired by other entrepreneurs and easily learn from them.

27. I easily learn from other business owners.

28. I am free to learn all I need to know in my business.

29. I choose to learn quickly and easily.

30. I love and accept my mind's natural ability to learn.

31. It is okay for me to want to learn more and grow.

32. It's easy for me to learn from others.

33. I quickly learn from all my business relationships.

34. I am clear about what I want from a coaching/mentoring relationship.

35. I feel safe and powerful when I outsource tasks in my business.

36. I rise to the challenge of technology and use it well.

37. I accept my imperfections as opportunities to learn valuable lessons in my life.

38. ______________________________

39. ______________________________

40. ______________________________

41. ______________________________

42. ______________________________

43. ______________________________

44. ______________________________

45. ______________________________

46. ______________________________

47. ______________________________

48. ______________________________

49. ______________________________

50. ______________________________

51. ______________________________

52. ______________________________

11

# LIFESTYLE

1. My business gives me the financial freedom to travel whenever I want.

2. I have a business and lifestyle that I love.

3. I experience freedom on a daily basis.

4. I'm doing what I always wanted, thanks to my business.

5. I make my dreams a reality and live my ultimate lifestyle.

6. I enjoy my business and I am fulfilled by the work that I do.

7. My business brings me great joy.

8. I contribute to the world in a meaningful way, and I am paid back a million-fold.

9. I choose a business that impacts this world in a positive way.

10. I have a happy life outside my business.

11. I can have a multimillion dollar/pound/euro business and still have plenty of free time.

12. It's possible for me to have a successful business and a good relationship with a man/woman.

13. It's easy for me to have a successful business and still have as much space and time for myself as I want.

14. Running my business is easy and nourishing.

15. I am grateful for the life and work that I do.

16. It's easy for me to upgrade the things I own to better quality items.

17. My ultimate lifestyle is easy to achieve.

18. It's easy for me to make time for self care.

19. I live a first class life and I offer a first class service to my clients.

20. I make enough money to have a weekly housekeeper.

21. My business allows me to live my life purpose.

22. My business allows me to express myself fully.

23. The Universe/God willingly helps me to create my ideal lifestyle.

24. I deserve to have the lifestyle I want.

25. It's safe and appropriate to have the lifestyle of my dreams.

26. I am free to create my ideal lifestyle.

27. I choose to have a vibrant, exciting life.

28. I see beauty in all parts of my life.

29. It's safe and appropriate for me to prioritize my own needs.

30. I take action to create my ideal lifestyle.

31. I build my ideal lifestyle in alignment with my inspired vision.

32. I am ready, willing, and able to create the life of my dreams.

33. It's easy for me to build my ultimate lifestyle.

34. I am worthy of living a satisfying, exciting life.

35. It's safe and appropriate for me to be free.

36. I make time to play in business and in life.

37. I easily find and connect with people who support my life of financial freedom.

38. I live in harmony with my business.

39. I live a happy, joyful, and prosperous life.

40. I live a healthy, wealthy, and enriched life.

41. I live an abundant and generous lifestyle.

42. It's easy for me to have fun.

43. It's easy for me to disconnect from work.

44. It's easy for me to go on holidays.

45. I live and travel with a first class mindset.

46. It's safe and appropriate to relax.

47. I protect myself with self care.

48. Self care is the best protection for me.

49. I easily attract all that I desire.

50. I live in a self-aware and fully autonomous way.

51. I live in a carefree manner because I know that everything is taken care of.

52. When I live trustingly, only good things happen to me.

53. I live a life of flow.

54. My life is full of grace and peace.

55. I slow down and see the beauty around me.

56. I savor and enjoy each moment.

57. I am happy in every moment of every day.

58. I am aware of life's everyday miracles.

59. I make space for quiet time in my life.

60. I am joyful about my present and my future.

61. Everything is in divine and perfect order, right now and always.

62. Everything I need is provided to me, always.

63. I allow myself all the quiet time I need.

64. I make quiet time a priority.

65. I take full responsibility for fulfilling my life and dreams.

66. It's easy for me to visualize the lifestyle of my dreams.

67. I value freedom and I feel it every day in my business.

68. I take good care of my body.

69. I feel pleasure and abundance with every breath I take.

70. I am very fortunate to work at what I love to do.

71. My life and business are an expression of my playful nature and I love them!

72. I connect easily and often to nature.

73. I am safe always, and I am loved.

74. I trust in the process of life.

75. I am deeply nourished by nature.

76. Abundance makes my life easier.

77. I graciously walk away from conflict.

78. I allow my mind to relax and be at peace.

79. The world is a safe place for me.

80. Surviving and thriving is easy and effortless for me.

81. It's easy for me to survive and thrive in this world.

82. I thrive the most when I work and exercise in a balanced way.

83. It's easy for me to work in a balanced way.

84. It's safe and appropriate for me to work in a balanced way.

85. It's easy for me to live a balanced life.

86. ______________________________

87. ______________________________

88. ______________________________

89. ______________________________

90. ______________________________

12

# MARKETING AND SALES

1. I receive regular invitations to speak.

2. I make sure every sale lays the foundation for the next sale.

3. I have a funnel filled with quality prospects and leads.

4. My profits increase weekly.

5. I turn every business transaction into one that is mutually beneficial for myself and for my clients.

6. I take action to build my online tribe via blogging and social media.

7. I enjoy business networking and I find it easy and effortless to network with others.

8. I always spot opportunities  to network for my business.

9. I am well connected with an extensive business network.

10. I am a skilled at selling my products and services to others.

11. It's okay for people to say no to me.

12. When I speak, my ideal clients feel compelled to sign up with me.

13. I am a fantastic sales person and my ideal clients say yes to working with me.

14. It energizes me to market myself and my business.

15. It's safe to be rejected.

16. It's easy for me to attract my target number of people for my programs and events.

17. It's easy to receive invitations to speaking opportunities.

18. I effectively and efficiently use social media to bring in paying clients.

19. I am a confident and engaging public speaker.

20. I easily accept opportunities to promote my business.

21. It's safe for people to say no to me.

22. It's okay when people reject my offerings.

23. Selling from speaking and webinars is easy and effortless for me.

24. I'm an excellent salesperson who always sells congruently.

25. I feel congruent and comfortable during sales conversations.

26. I am in control of my sales process.

27. I have a structured sales conversation that I effortlessly guide people through.

28. I am clear about the unique benefits to the products and services that I offer.

29. I believe that my products and services can make a difference to my ideal clients.

30. I have a clear vision of who my ideal client is and what s/he is like.

31. I create a good first impression whenever I meet people online and offline.

32. I love networking to meet new people and get new clients.

33. Potential clients feel certainty and safety when speaking to me about my offerings.

34. I clearly communicate the value of my products and services.

35. I am comfortable being a salesperson.

36. I am comfortable selling my products and services.

37. It's easy and comfortable for me to express who I am in my business.

38. It's safe and appropriate for me and my business to take up space.

39. I feel comfortable and confident delivering powerful content via webinar.

40. It's easy for me to invest in marketing my business.

41. It's easy for me to be consistent in my marketing.

42. I easily write and send weekly newsletters to my list.

43. I easily and clearly express the value of all my offerings.

44. It's safe and appropriate for people to question my prices.

45. I easily call people into my orbit.

46. People understand me.

47. I love [doing videos/recording podcast episodes/writing blog posts] for my business.

48. It's easy for me to batch and release [videos/podcast episodes/blog posts] for my business.

49. It's easy for me to fit [videos/podcast episodes/blog posts] into my schedule.

50. Building a thriving [YouTube channel/podcast/blog/Facebook group/etc.] is important to the success of my business.

51. I have a super successful [YouTube channel/podcast/blog/etc.] with tens of thousands of subscribers.

52. I'm skilled at setting up powerful Facebook ads that abundantly feed my sales funnels.

53. I regularly write guest blog posts for other people to increase my reach.

54. I have an eager team of affiliates who promote my work for a commission.

55. My gorgeous website clearly reflects the power of the work I do.

56. My powerful website regularly fills my sales funnels with clients.

57. I have an active and engaged email list of people who love my work.

58. I have an easy to manage editorial calendar for my content.

59. Sales conversations are easy and fun for me.

60. I get excited for my sales conversations.

61. Marketing is fun and enjoyable for me.

62. ______________________________

63. ______________________________

64. ______________________________

65. ______________________________

66. ______________________________

67. ______________________________

68. ______________________________

69. ______________________________

70. ______________________________

13

## MONEY

1. Money is Divine.

2. I am spiritually and financially rich.

3. Money flows to me regularly and consistently.

4. I'm responsible with money and I run a profitable business.

5. I have all the money I need and more.

6. I'm great at saving and investing money.

7. Money flows to me in amounts greater than my need.

8. I have a great relationship with money.

9. It's easy for me to make a lot of money.

10. It's okay to spend money.

11. I focus only on what's important to enable money to come to me easily.

12. It's easy for me to receive.

13. I know what's important and effective to enable money to come to me easily.

14. I love money and money loves me.

15. I am financially independent and I love it.

16. I am relaxed about money.

17. The more money I have, the more money I have to give.

18. I appreciate and value money.

19. I always have more money than I need.

20. I can be trusted with money.

21. I trust the Universe/God to provide for me.

22. It's easy for me to bring in money during my transition period.

23. I have an abundance of resources available to me.

24. I live in a world of plenty.

25. I trust that money comes when I want it.

26. It's safe for me to be wealthy and use my money for the highest good.

27. I constantly attract more abundance.

28. It's easy for me to get paid for my knowledge.

29. Money comes to me easily and effortlessly.

30. I love money and I believe that money is important.

31. I enjoy abundance and plenty.

32. I love feeling wealthy.

33. I am financially responsible.

34. I am great at managing my money and making it multiply.

35. I am financially successful.

36. Money can come to me in fun ways.

37. I am financially independent.

38. I transform and manifest my financial reality.

39. I am responsible for my financial situation.

40. I do good things with the money I make: I donate 10% of income to Kiva, I save 10% for investments, and I spend 10% on fun things.

41. I have enough money to reinvest in my business to help it grow.

42. I am a magnet for money and success.

43. It's safe and appropriate to make a lot of money quickly and easily.

44. It's easy for me to make money when I'm having fun.

45. It's safe and appropriate for me to receive large sums of money.

46. Creating revenue is easy and I have zero debt.

47. I always have more than enough money to pay my rent and my bills.

48. I can make all the money I want from my business.

49. Money is good, and I love it!

50. I deserve money and I always have more than enough.

51. The Universe/God is constantly magnetizing money to me.

52. I receive my wealth and abundance with ease, grace, and gratitude.

53. It's safe and appropriate for me to ask for the money I want in exchange for my services.

54. More money helps me to make a difference in the world.

55. It's safe and appropriate for me to make money in my business, even when other people are in need.

56. It's easy for me to remember to track all the money that comes to me.

57. It's easy for me to save money.

58. It's safe and appropriate for me to check my bank balance on a regular basis.

59. It's easy for me to live a debt-free life.

60. I trust myself to be responsible with my money.

61. Money is a way for me to make a difference in the world by helping others.

62. The more money I have, the more people I can help.

63. It's safe and appropriate for me to have more money than I need.

64. I am free to want money.

65. I choose to live a wealthy life.

66. I love and accept my bank account, no matter what the balance is.

67. I am grateful for the money I do have.

68. I release my painful money story and eagerly look forward to money flowing into my life.

69. Although I grieve for money I have lost, I am trusting and confident that more money is coming to me.

70. I forgive myself for how I handle money, and I trust myself to manage money sensibly.

71. I bless and release all those who have caused me financial distress.

72. It's easy for me to say no, even when money is involved.

73. I have the freedom to change my prices whenever I want.

74. It's safe and appropriate for me to receive money for doing what I love.

75. I generate enough income that being in business is worthwhile for me.

76. It's safe and appropriate for me to charge more for my services than other people.

77. My business consistently supports me in ever increasing amounts.

78. I open myself up to receive money and abundance.

79. I am worthy of receiving money and abundance.

80. Money is safe.

81. I make and sustain wealth easily.

82. I can help others more if I meet my own needs first.

83. I am talented with money and investments.

84. I look after my money wisely.

85. I always make more money than I need from my work.

86. It's easy for me to set and achieve challenging money goals.

87. Making money is a priority for me.

88. I easily pay off my credit cards in full every month.

89. I have a savings account with lots of money in it.

90. It's easy for me to keep money in my bank account.

91. It's easy for me to live a debt-free life.

92. I am financially savvy.

93. I easily handle my own finances.

94. I keep on top of all my bookkeeping and taxes.

95. I love looking at my bank account.

96. It's safe and appropriate for me to charge whatever prices I want.

97. It's safe and appropriate for me to trust my prices.

98. I can be trusted with lots and lots of money.

99. I can be trusted with millions of pounds/dollars/euros.

100. My natural relationship with money is responsible.

101. The more freedom I feel, the more money I make.

102. The more I travel, the more money I make.

103. I easily resolve any money problems by getting more clients.

104. I deserve more money.

105. I have an intrinsic ability to increase my wealthy by being me and sharing my message.

106. It's easy for me to imagine receiving large amounts of money.

107. It's easy for me to receive large amounts of money.

108. It's easy for me to support myself financially.

109. I am ready to have all the riches I desire.

110. I am open to receive all the money I need to be free.

111. I easily maintain and grow my income while doing deep healing work.

112. ____________________

113. ____________________

114. ____________________

115. ____________________

116. ____________________

117. ____________________

118. ____________________

119. ____________________

120. ____________________

121. ____________________

122. ____________________

123. ____________________

124. ____________________

125. ____________________

126. ____________________

14

## PERSONAL POWER

1. I stand authentically in my power.

2. I'm safe and powerful in the world.

3. I express my personal power in everything I do in my business.

4. I have a deep belief in my own personal power and my ability to help people.

5. I take the initiative to create my life the way I want it.

6. I have the power to make my vision and dreams come true.

7. I am true to my personal vision and I take action toward it.

8. I easily speak my personal truth with clarity and confidence.

9. Taking action when I'm afraid gives me power.

10. I give myself permission to do what I love and want.

11. I accept and cherish the power within me.

12. I make a difference in the world.

13. I have a powerful personality and people are attracted to me.

14. I have the power to realize my life purpose through my business.

15. I trust every business decision that I make.

16. I trust my ability to make good decisions for my business and life.

17. I accept and embrace the power within me.

18. I easily and effortlessly take charge in my life.

19. I am in full control of my mind, my body, and my life.

20. When I take responsibility for my life, my sense of personal power grows.

21. I am comfortable and powerful in my own skin.

22. I am in charge of my own life.

23. I am powerful and decisive in all that I do.

24. I have the power to take care of myself.

25. My personal power helps me to easily change and adapt when needed.

26. My sense of personal power is soft and flowing.

27. I feel a strong connection to my personal power.

28. I work to my strengths, and this increases my personal power.

29. I quickly and easily get help to support my weaknesses, and this makes me stronger.

30. I feel a strong sense of courage and conviction.

31. I own my personal power and I take responsibility for everything I experience.

32. I take responsibility for my life experience.

33. My clear sense of personal power is attractive to others.

34. It feels strong and powerful to be me.

35. I easily step into my power and express myself.

36. It's safe for me to take radical actions in my business.

37. I have the power to stand my own in the face of disagreement.

38. I kindly and easily speak my truth at all times.

39. I have permission to be different.

40. My power is in my differences.

41. I am assertive in all domains of my business and life.

42. I have the power to change.

43. It's easy for me to say no when other people want things from me.

44. It's easy for me to ask for what I need.

45. I live with faith, courage, and strength.

46. When I put myself first, I can handle anything that comes my way.

47. I always put my own needs first.

48. I trust I always make the best decisions for me.

49. I remain calm and grounded at all times.

50. I easily create and uphold boundaries that allow me to elevate myself.

51. I'm capable of being powerful.

52. I'm worthy of being powerful.

53. I'm ready, willing, and able to be powerful.

54. People trust me.

55. I have powerful energy.

56. My energy comes through in a big way.

57. I own my powerful energy.

58. I am strong, powerful, and grounded in every way.

59. It's easy for me to step into a higher vibration of energy.

60. Boundaries can be gentle and calm.

61. I am intuitively open to my deepest self.

62. I am deeply and firmly rooted in myself.

63. I am fully present and grounded in my body.

64. I know I am protected, now and always.

65. I take full responsibility for my life.

66. I easily step into my greatness.

67. People want to be in my presence.

68. I walk through the world with my stage energy.

69. I am a conduit for the Divine.

70. I embody the fullness of all that I am.

71. I have what it takes to do this work.

72. My humor makes me approachable.

73. When I use humor it's a magnet for people.

74. I embody my stage energy every day.

75. I speak my truth easily and transparently.

76. I am a visionary.

77. I am powerful and strong.

78. I am all that I need.

79. All that I need is within me.

80. I easily tap into the knowledge of the universe and allow myself to receive.

81. I easily create miracles in my life.

82. I am ready, willing, and able to receive miracles in my life.

83. I am fully coherent in all that I do.

84. My true self is awake and alive.

85. I know exactly who my true self is.

86. I live my true self every day of my life.

87. I have strong and healthy boundaries.

88. I am a divine being of light.

89. I am present in my body and all is well.

90. I fully claim my whole, brilliant self.

91. I fully step into my brilliant magnificence.

92. It's easy for me to shine, light up, and just go for it.

93. I easily open up to and connect with my complete self.

94. I fully embrace my superpowers.

95. I am a limitless expression of [God's/the goddess's/the Universe's/etc.] love.

96. ______________________________

97. ______________________________

98. ______________________________

99. ______________________________

100. ______________________________

101. ______________________________

102. ______________________________

103. ______________________________

104. ______________________________

105. ______________________________

106. ______________________________

107. ______________________________

108. ______________________________

109. ______________________________

110. ______________________________

15

## STRATEGY, CLARITY AND VISION

1. I have a clear business plan.

2. I have brilliant business ideas.

3. I can overcome any challenge in my business.

4. I am decisive rather than doubtful.

5. I have a killer business idea that appeals to my ideal clients, and I know what that is.

6. I have clear plans for revenue streams that clients want.

7. I have a clear business model that people want now.

8. I make decisions based on my values.

9. It's easy for me to imagine a business model that is fun.

10. I have a clear vision for my business which is aligned with my purpose.

11. I see clear and obvious signs that guide me along my path.

12. I have a clear marketing strategy for my business and I'm fully confident that it works.

13. I let go of the need for approval from others and I do what I think is right in my business.

14. It's easy and effortless to realize my vision.

15. Creating my global vision is stress free.

16. I have absolute clarity on how to run my business.

17. I'm clear about what I want in my business and I follow my intuition.

18. My mind is calm and clear.

19. It's easy for me to see the highest priorities in my life and business.

20. Everything I need to know is clearly revealed to me.

21. My vision for my business is based on my life purpose.

22. I have a clear vision on how I want to run my business.

23. My divine wisdom guides my clear vision.

24. My inner vision is always clear and focused.

25. It's easy for me to see the signs that mark my journey through life and business.

26. I easily create a business I love to look at.

27. I feel blessed with absolute clarity.

28. My purpose is clear and I can see my path open before me.

29. I clearly see my gifts, skills, and abilities and I offer them through my business.

30. My mind is clear and focused.

31. I can see clearly now and I take steps down my path.

32. My life purpose is clear to me, and I easily follow it.

33. The bigger I believe, the bigger I achieve.

34. I easily see the next step toward my goals, and I take it.

35. I invest in the best business mentors and coaches to help me grow my business.

36. I have a clear plan for business success.

37. It's safe and appropriate for me to focus on my highest path.

38. I have absolute clarity about what I'm doing and offering in my business.

39. It's easy for me to turn my business ideas into money-making products and services.

40. I feel abundant regardless of how much money is in my bank account.

41. I have a variety of passive income streams in my business.

42. I feel comfortable taking risks in business and in life.

43. I am naturally insightful and innovative.

44. It's safe and appropriate for me to invest in my business.

45. My beliefs and my actions shape my business.

46. I always know the right time to launch a new product.

47. All of my skills are coming together into a cohesive vision.

48. It's easy for me to be organized in my business.

49. I'm organized and prepared well in advance for my webinars and workshops.

50. It's easy for me to know what I want, to ask for it, and to have it.

51. My life is full of ease and flow.

52. My business is full of ease and flow.

53. I have multiple highly successful sales funnels.

54. I have a clear understanding of how to create the right sales funnels for my business.

55. My vision and mindset are constantly upleveling.

56. I am clear in my message.

57. I easily make play a part of my work.

58. My work is fun and playful.

59. Negotiating is easy for me.

60. I feel good about backing out of responsibilities that no longer serve me.

61. I choose my own direction resolutely.

62. I have patience as my dreams come together.

63. I enjoy the process of realizing my dreams.

64. I feel gratitude every step of the way.

65. I open myself up to receive big downloads.

66. I give myself the time and space to receive big downloads.

67. I know where I'm going at all times.

68. I easily see the next step on my journey.

69. I let go of all my fears as I take big steps forward.

70. I have an open mind and am ready for downloads.

71. I know exactly what makes my heart sing.

72. I know exactly what I want to get out of my life.

73. I know exactly what it is that I want to do with my business.

74. I know my calling and the work I am supposed to do in my life.

75. I always know what to do in any situation.

76. I celebrate my knowledge and I allow myself to think whatever I want to think.

77. I let my thoughts soar high.

78. When faced with an obstacle, I easily flow around it.

79. I know I can easily overcome any obstacle in life and business.

80. It's easy for me to find simple solutions to complicated problems.

81. I observe everything that happens in a state of peace and nonattachment.

82. Clarity and harmony are within me and around me, and all is well.

83. I easily check in with my soul and see who I am.

84. ______________________________

85. ______________________________

86. ______________________________

87. ______________________________

88. ______________________________

89. ______________________________

90. ______________________________

16

## SUCCESS AND OPPORTUNITIES

1. I am extraordinarily successful on my own terms.

2. It's safe and appropriate for me to be successful.

3. I appreciate the success I have.

4. I feel safe and successful now.

5. I am confident in my success.

6. I appreciate my success.

7. I am comfortable with my own success.

8. I accept how successful I am.

9. I am good enough to be successful.

10. I have a wildly successful business.

11. I am a successful entrepreneur.

12. My experience and expertise help me to be successful.

13. I am disciplined and determined to succeed.

14. The important people in my life will support me in my success.

15. It's safe and appropriate for me to share my business successes.

16. It's easy for me to succeed in life and business.

17. Success means acting with integrity and making a difference.

18. I choose to be successful in my business and I am open to it.

19. I am safe even when people feel threatened by my success.

20. My true friends support me in my success.

21. I am wildly successful beyond my dreams.

22. I enjoy experiencing unexpected successes and pleasant surprises.

23. I embrace opportunity and abundance in my business.

24. New opportunities come easily to me.

25. Opportunities for financial growth continue to come my way.

26. My business is full of opportunities.

27. I am a full time, successful entrepreneur.

28. I am a best-selling author whose books drive clients to my business.

29. Having a business coach/mentor helps my business be successful.

30. It's easy for me to talk about my successes with others.

31. I feel confident and deserving when sharing my successes.

32. I am deserving of success.

33. I love feeling successful.

34. I feel joyously successful.

35. I am free to have sustainable success in my business and life.

36. Business success is easy and natural for me.

37. I am happy with where I am right now in my business.

38. I am inspired by other entrepreneurs in my field.

39. I am a successful and inspired entrepreneur.

40. It's safe for myself and others to see my full potential.

41. It's safe for me to realize my full potential.

42. It's easy for me to realize my full potential.

43. I achieve all my goals easily and rapidly.

44. I achieve greatness and success.

45. I give myself permission to celebrate my own successes.

46. I am grateful for all I have and for all I receive.

47. I notice and embrace the new opportunities that are now in my life.

48. I always balance giving and receiving.

49. It's easy for me to reward myself for my work.

50. I magnetically attract success, wealth, and opportunities.

51. I achieve something extraordinary every day.

52. My business takes off like a rocket.

53. I successfully grow my business and I am compensated for my efforts.

54. My clear intuition drives my business success.

55. The more I act on my intuition, the more success I enjoy.

56. My success is linked to my ability to be me.

57. The more I am me, the more abundance I enjoy.

58. I relax into the feeling of abundance and allow it to magnify easily.

59. The more I listen to my intuition, the more I increase my abundance.

60. I relax into creating abundance in ways that are easy and fun.

61. I enjoy the process of realizing my dreams.

62. I am ready, willing, and able to embrace success in my life and business now.

63. I am ready for success.

64. I am ready, willing, and able to embrace all opportunities in my life and business.

65. I say yes to opportunities, even when they seem scary.

66. I open myself up to receive success and opportunity in my life and business now.

67. ______________________________

68. ______________________________

69. ______________________________

70. ______________________________

71. ______________________________

17

# VALUE AND SELF WORTH

1. I am worthy of happiness, and success.

2. I have something valuable to offer the world.

3. I'm worthy of achieving my business goals.

4. I value my products and services and what I have to offer.

5. I have something wonderful to offer the world.

6. I have valuable knowledge and skills that I apply to my business.

7. I fully embrace all the knowledge and experience I got from [previous company/business].

8. I already know everything I need to start my own business.

9. I'm worthy of working with clients with more money than me.

10. I'm worthy of working with wealthy, successful people regardless of my income.

11. I am good enough.

12. I deeply appreciate and accept myself.

13. I am unique and I love my uniqueness.

14. My message is valuable and people want to learn from me.

15. I'm good enough in every way.

16. I see the value in what I have to offer and I easily communicate it to others.

17. I am good enough and I am confident in all kinds of business company.

18. I value myself and my connection to Source.

19. I deserve good things in my life.

20. I am happy with the way I am.

21. It's okay for me to be myself.

22. I always have something valuable to offer.

23. I am innately valuable.

24. I am a [wo]man of immense talent.

25. I am worthy of having a successful business.

26. My knowledge is extremely valuable and people pay me for it.

27. It's safe for me to be myself in my business.

28. It's easy for me to be authentic in my business

29. I am unique in my own way and I am the only one who can offer what I do how I do.

30. I let go of self criticism and replace it with self acceptance.

31. I am free to be me and to run my business how I want.

32. My story is important and so am I.

33. I am a unique, special, creative, and wonderful person.

34. I am worthy of serving myself and others.

35. I am worthy of this successful business and life.

36. It's safe and appropriate to be myself and to believe in myself.

37. I am proud of who I am.

38. I am thankful for the advantages that I have.

39. I am grateful for who I am.

40. I value the contribution I make in the world.

41. I have valuable things to say that can help people.

42. My ideal clients want to hear what I have to say.

43. I already know enough and I have enough experience to serve my clients well.

44. I am complete as I am.

45. I fully step into the value that I bring to my business.

46. The person I look up to and respect the most in the world is me.

47. I am my biggest fan.

48. I attract only the people who can see the value in and benefit from my work.

49. I value the characteristics that make me different.

50. I am enough.

51. I deserve to be massively successful.

52. I make a unique and specific contribution.

53. It's easy for other people to see the value of my contribution.

54. I'm already more than qualified to do the work I do.

55. I'm already ready.

56. I have the ability to help so many people.

57. It's safe and appropriate for me to be myself.

58. It's safe and appropriate for me to be unexpectedly different.

59. I deeply and completely accept myself for who I am.

60. I firmly believe in and express my worth.

61. I have a deep inner awareness and confidence in my self worth.

62. I have unwavering confidence in the value I offer.

63. I have unwavering confidence in all my pricing.

64. I am worthy of charging whatever prices I want.

65. My time and experience are valuable.

66. I'm clear about the value of my work and I consistently attract the right clients to me.

67. It's easy for me to truly accept all of who I am, and I do.

68. I am worthy of people showing up for who I am.

69. My realness is one of my most beautiful aspects.

70. I appreciate all the work that I do.

71. I deserve miracles.

72. I am fully qualified to know what I know.

73. I give myself my own stamp of approval.

74. I am good enough, qualified enough, and official enough.

75. I am perfectly acceptable just as I am today.

76. I easily see and experience the fullness of my gifts.

77. I easily accept myself and others, free from judgement.

78. I'm wise enough to do all the things I want to do.

79. It's safe to be me, just as I am.

80. I am smart enough to be famous.

81. I am worthy to be prosperous.

82. I am trained enough to do all that I want to do.

83. ______________________________

84. ______________________________

85. ______________________________

86. ______________________________

87. ______________________________

88. ______________________________

89. ______________________________

90. ______________________________

18

# VISIBILITY

1. It's safe and appropriate for me to stand out and be visible.

2. I love standing out from the crowd like a tall poppy.

3. It's safe to stand out in new ways.

4. I feel comfortable being different from others.

5. I feel safe being different from other entrepreneurs.

6. It's safe and appropriate for me to be a business star.

7. I am ready to be seen both online and offline.

8. It's easy and effortless for me to claim my space in the world.

9. It's safe for me to be seen anywhere.

10. It's easy for me to share value on video.

11. My stories show people what's possible for them.

12. It's easy to make myself heard and participate in groups.

13. It's safe and comfortable for me to be visible and in the spotlight.

14. I feel confident and happy with myself when people look at me.

15. I am ready to put myself out there with my new business.

16. I am safe even if I have online haters and trolls.

17. People find it easy to find me because I am easily accessible both online and offline.

18. It's easy for me to speak up spontaneously.

19. It's safe and appropriate for me to be the center of attention.

20. I am a natural on camera and people love my videos.

21. It's safe to stand out and be an expert in my field.

22. I feel confident when filming videos and it's easy for me to watch myself on video.

23. It's okay to be out there in front of people telling my story.

24. It's safe and appropriate for me to shine online.

25. It's safe for me to shine my light out into the world.

26. I love the feeling of shining like a star.

27. I am inspired by the accomplishments of others, and others are inspired by mine.

28. I naturally find it easy to be visible, even in new situations.

29. My timing in my videos is impeccable, and I always know what to say.

30. I deeply appreciate and accept my efforts to be more visible with my business.

31. I am proud of how my visibility has increased both online and offline.

32. I accept my imperfections in my writing and my videos.

33. It's easy for me to create inspiring, popular videos.

34. I allow myself to be vulnerable in my writing and my videos.

35. It's easy for me to express my uniqueness online.

36. I have a large audience which listens to what I have to say.

37. It's safe and appropriate for me to be me and to express who I am.

38. It's my purpose to show up in the world and share my story.

39. I am seen and valued for my expertise.

40. I'm seen and acknowledged for my achievements.

41. It's my time to be in the spotlight, and I'm ready for it.

42. My audience is ready for me to put this out in a big way.

43. I inspire people all over the world with my work.

44. I am a big business celebrity with a raving tribe of fans.

45. I speak with clarity and strength.

46. I shine my light out into the world and attract my ideal clients.

47. I have a thriving online tribe of people who jump to buy my things.

48. I'm fully comfortable in the spotlight.

49. I'm ready, willing, and able to receive judgement.

50. I love pitching myself for PR and media opportunities because it gets me clients.

51. I love being visible with my business.

52. I enjoy publicly celebrating my accomplishments.

53. It's easy for me to share my accomplishments with others.

54. It's easy for me to speak up and ask questions.

55. I express myself fully in a loving way.

56. I easily bring out those things that are most profound inside me.

57. It's easy for me to outwardly express and externalize my divinity.

58. I'm safe when I'm tall and elevated.

59. I'm safe when I ascend to a high space.

60. I am here to be big and visible.

61. My divine mission is to help people on a global level.

62. I stand out energetically in a very big way.

63. My destiny is to stand out globally.

64. People want to hear what I have to say.

65. I own my presence on a big stage.

66. I claim my space on the big stage.

67. I expand my vision globally.

68. I embody all of who I am when I am on stage.

69. I'm a great podcast guest that everyone wants to interview.

70. It's easy for me to be accepted as a guest on other podcasts.

71. People love it when I show up as my unique self.

72. It's safe and appropriate for people to disagree with me.

73. It's safe and appropriate for people to criticize me.

74. It's safe and appropriate for me to speak my truth.

75. It's safe and appropriate for me to be powerful and known.

76. I have a steady stream of media outlets approaching me.

77. The media sees me as an expert in [your field of expertise].

78. I am famous for [your field of expertise].

79. I am THE go-to person for [your field of expertise].

80. I clearly express myself openly.

81. People flock to hear me, see me, and be in my tribe.

82. It's safe and appropriate for me to be different.

83. I easily radiate my gifts out to the world.

84. I give myself permission to share my gifts far and wide.

85. I easily speak up and express myself fully.

86. I share my message in a way that's aligned with my higher self.

87. It's safe and appropriate for me to share what I know with the world.

88. I easily radiate my brilliance as a messenger of truth.

89. It's safe and appropriate for me to reveal the brilliance of my light.

90. I easily easily show up in the fullest expression of myself.

91. I easily allow myself to take up space to shine.

92. The more I shine my light, the more I connect with others.

93. It's easy for me to radiate brilliance and vulnerability.

94. It's easy for me to connect with my audience and expand my reach.

95. I am loved, noticed, and appreciated.

96. I am ready, willing, and able to be seen.

97. I am ready, willing, and able to take up space.

98. I am ready, willing, and able to appear regularly in people's timelines.

99. It's easy for me to build a thriving community, both online and offline.

100. Speaking opportunities come to me easily and regularly.

101. ______________________________

102. ______________________________

103. ______________________________

104. ______________________________

105. ______________________________

106. ______________________________

107. ______________________________

108. ______________________________

109. ______________________________

# 19

# HOW TO CREATE YOUR OWN BELIEF STATEMENTS

You'll notice that I've left plenty of lines within each category for you to create your own belief statements. This is important: while the belief statements I've included here cover a wide variety of situations, invariably your situation will be different and you'll want or need to believe certain things that I haven't covered here. That's when it's time to create your own statements from scratch.

The important thing when creating belief statements is that you use language that feels and sounds right to you. They need to be meaningful, and they need to sound like something that you would say or write. This means that you'll probably want to adapt some of the statements on the previous lists to suit your style, and you'll most likely want to create brand new statements at some point. Here's how you can do that.

## The quick way

First, take a look at where you are in your business and life, and ask yourself some questions. What are you currently experiencing? What's currently going on that you don't like? What are you afraid of? What are you procrastinating on?

Next, flip the issue on its head and ask yourself some more questions. What would you rather have instead? How do you want things to be? What do you need to believe to have this? Who do you need to be to achieve this?

From there, create your new belief statements around what you *do* want. These statements should adhere to the following criteria:

1. **First person.** You want to speak in terms of what *you* want: "I am good enough as I am."

2. **Present tense.** Your subconscious mind lives in the present, so avoid speaking about the past or the future. Again, "I am good enough." Not, "I will be good enough after I finish my training course."

**3. Positive.** You want to focus on what you *do* want, and not on what you *don't* want. "I am good enough." Not: "I don't feel inferior to others."

**4. Concise.** The statements need to be short and easy to remember. If you find yourself creating long, difficult statements, try to find a way to split each statement into two parts. "I am good enough." Not: "I let go of my need for perfection and I am good enough in every single way, and I wake up feeling excited to be my unique self every single morning." Try memorizing that one, and then repeating it over and over again. Not easy!

Let's focus on doing things the easy way. Split that goal up into three parts: "I let go of my need for perfection." "I am good enough in every single way." "I wake up feeling excited to be my unique self every single morning."

Remember: the processes and techniques I've recommended are fast and easy. It's better to split a complex statement into thirds and spend five minutes reprogramming each of the three beliefs than it is to create one giant, awkward belief that you struggle with.

**5. Emotional.** Focus on creating statements about topics or issues that you're really passionate about. "I am good enough" may or may not be exciting to you, even if it sounds like a great thing to believe. Perhaps you would be better off re-wording the belief to something like "I'm blessed and grateful to be me." Or "I love myself just as I am." Or "I deeply and completely love and accept myself for who I am." Use your own words to make it meaningful.

**6. Language.** Again, the statement needs to be in your words. This is slightly related to the previous point, so if "I am good enough" is not the kind of language that you would use, adjust the statement to something similar, like "I value myself as I am today." Also, if English is not your native language, or it's not the language you think in or use in your everyday life, consider translating the statements into whatever language you prefer.

The last two points go for every single belief statement in this book as well. If you come across a statement that you like, but it doesn't feel quite right, take a minute to re-word it so that it feels really exciting to you. Also, if a concept sounds good, but it uses language that you wouldn't normally use, re-work the statement so that it sounds like something you would actually say or write.

This is all about *you*, and what statements are best for *you*. That should be clear by now, but I feel the need to repeat myself (again). You know best.

## The deeper process

Sometimes we can benefit from going even deeper to get our belief statements. Years ago, I created a signature program to help you take a good look at who you are, where you are in your business and life, and where you're going. These three areas will help you to dig deeper and get a clear vision and feeling for what you want in your business and life, and what your blocks are. In this program, I walk you through a clear system to answer these three questions and to help you get absolute clarity.

While it's not currently available as an online program, I've got many blog posts on the topic (which I call The Three Questions), as well as several podcast episodes.

Here's what it looks like, step by step:

1. Who am I?
2. Where am I?
3. Where am I going?
4. Inner work
5. Action plan

* * *

## Other ways

There are plenty of other ways to get creative and write your own belief statements that are meaningful to you. Here are some other ways I do it:

- Weekly Akashic records emails. I regularly subscribe to Vickie Young's weekly, personalized messages from my Records Keepers, and they've been very helpful in keeping me on track and stretching myself into new levels. When I receive my weekly email, I print it out and paste it in my journal, where I journal on the topic. I often create belief statements around the topic of the email, to help me fully embrace the content of the message.
- Journaling. I often write in my journal about things that I'm experiencing, things I want to achieve, and how I want to grow. From these journal entries, I create belief statements that will help me to achieve my goals.
- Sessions with my business mentor. I get so much out of each session with Lisa Wechtenhiser that I end up with at least eight pages of notes from each hour-long session. From there, I go through the notes and create belief statements to support the things I need to believe so I can take action and work on the things that came up in each session.

- Pay attention throughout your work day to the things you hesitate doing. Look at the things you're procrastinating on, and write them down. I used to keep a small notebook next to my computer to write down everything that came up for me during the day, and in the evening I would spend some time doing the mindset work to change my beliefs around those areas.

20

## MOVING FORWARD

I hope you've found this workbook to be useful. I've tried to keep it simple, using the fifteen categories of business beliefs as a way to delve deeper into your mindset. Awareness is the first step to upgrading your business mindset, and the deeper you go, the easier it will be for you to get to the root of the issues that you want to shift.

If you're in any way hesitant to do this deep work, think about the following questions (and write down your answers).

What is it costing you to avoid doing this deep mindset work?

It's so easy to put off and just keep doing what you've been doing. But what will your business be like six months from now if you don't take new and different actions?

What will your business be like in six months, one year, or five years if you don't change your mindset and shift your limiting beliefs?

It's time to let those mind gremlins out of their cage, where they're trapped in your subconscious mind. Get them down on paper right here in this workbook so you can see them. Only once you're aware of them can you do something about them. And remember: it's easy to change your mindset. You just need to do the work.

## Take action today

Are you wondering exactly what you need to do now? I've broken it all down into five easy action steps. Transforming our mindset is easy, but it isn't exactly magic. It does require an investment of time and action, and sometimes money.

Here's how to get started:

1. Identify the core beliefs that you need to shift
2. Find the best process/technique for *you*
3. Find the best practitioner or facilitator for *you*
4. Do the inner work
5. Take action

## 1. Identify the beliefs you need

Identify the core beliefs that you need to shift in your business mindset, using the methods described in this workbook (muscle testing on the belief statements).

## 2 & 3. Find the best technique and practitioner

This may involve trial and error, as will finding the best practitioner or facilitator for you. If something doesn't feel quite right, then don't go back for another session. Listen to your gut feeling on this, and if you don't see changes fairly soon after your first session or sessions, you might want to reevaluate whether you've found the best method (or practitioner) for you.

After hearing so many great things about PSYCH-K®, I was tremendously disappointed in the first facilitator I saw. It was a terrible session, and I never went back to see her again. I then sought out another facilitator, but she convinced me to try ThetaHealing® instead, which I did enjoy, but I still wasn't working with the process that I wanted to try. Finally, just a week or so before training in the PSYCH-K® Basic Workshop, I found a facilitator I liked and had an excellent session with her.

The point of this story is that there are many processes and techniques out there, and there are many practitioners out there. Sometimes it can be tricky to find what's right for you. It can take trial and error.

There are many ways to reprogram your subconscious beliefs, some of which I've already mentioned earlier this book: Heart-centered Energy Work®, PSYCH-K®, ThetaHealing®, Emotional Freedom Techniques® (EFT or tapping), NLP (Neuro-Linguistic Programming), TAT (Tapas Acupressure Technique), Ask & Receive, hypnotherapy, and more. I've also experienced sound therapy sessions and light language sessions. In 2019, I graduated from a Shamanic Plant Spirit Healing Apprenticeship, which does exactly what it says in the name: it taught me how to work with plant spirits for healing (which, of course, can also help with limiting beliefs).

Change can be *very* quick when you're working at the subconscious level, so there's no need to attend weekly sessions for months before seeing results. Stay alert, and pay attention to how your life and business are different since you started doing the mindset work. Sometimes big changes occur, but people don't notice them, because things are going well and they're no longer experiencing whatever it was that they wanted to let go of. That's why it's so useful to write things down in a journal.

## 4. Do the training yourself

I always recommend that people train in a process or technique themselves so they can do the work on their own. There is great power in being able to transform your own beliefs whenever you want, wherever you want, however you want. I have spent the past several years working on my beliefs on a regular basis (at least once a week!), and I also see other professionals from time to time. In my experience, this is the perfect combination to approach changing our business beliefs.

If you've tried a number of different processes or techniques with other practitioners, you may have found one that you especially enjoy or that gets you great results. Train in it. Learn how to do it for yourself. This will require an initial investment, but it will save you time and money in the long run. You'll be able to make big changes in your belief system, and you'll be reaping the results in your business. This is what I mean when I say "do the inner work."

## 5. Take inspired action

When I work with clients, I always help them create a short action plan at the end of each session. This is important: no matter how much work we do to transform our beliefs and our mindset, we also have to take practical action. We can change all the beliefs we want, but if we don't actually *do the work* in our business, we won't magically create change.

We still need to write the blog posts, do the videos, market our business online, and have the sales calls.

I always say this is like climbing a spiral staircase: the left step is the mindset work, the right step is the practical action. Left, right, left, right, and up we go as we build our business.

In the next section, I talk a little bit about how you can work with me or with others if you feel drawn to do so. If not, I encourage you to read through it anyway, so you can at least have some point of comparison to other professionals that you may choose to work with. It helps to have an idea of how different people work so you can find what's best for you.

Remember . . . *you* know what's best for you! There's a reason I keep saying this: we can have the tendency to give our power away to others, but deep down, you're the one who knows what's best. Go with your gut feeling or with whatever your heart says. That's your higher self checking in with you to let you know which option is best.

# APPENDIX I

HOW TO COMMUNICATE WITH YOUR SUBCONSCIOUS MIND

## Muscle testing

There are many ways to communicate with the subconscious mind, but hypnosis is probably the best known method for obtaining information from it. While hypnosis can be incredibly powerful and life-changing, there are faster, simpler, and easier methods. (But again—use the technique that works for *you*.)

In my experience, the quickest and easiest way to communicate with the subconscious mind is through muscle testing. Muscle testing is an easy way for us to connect directly with our own subconscious or with other people's subconscious minds (in the case of working with a client). The theory behind muscle testing is that when the mind is holding a stressful thought or belief, a conflict is created in the brain, and this produces a weak response in the body. You may have seen people do muscle testing by pressing down on another person's outstretched arm.

I've learned many different ways of doing this over the years, and I used it a lot in the process that I previously worked with to help clients (and myself) with changing subconscious beliefs. The trick is to find the best method for *you*, when doing self muscle testing, and the best method for your *partner/client*, when you're working with others. In this chapter, I provide a quick explanation of how to use muscle testing both with yourself and with someone else, but you may find it easiest to refer to my video on the topic, which is available on my YouTube channel.

## Muscle testing with a partner

For muscle testing with a partner, the arm is generally used. The partner or client will hold their arm out to the front or to the side, and the other person will press down on the arm as the first person resists the pressure. The instructions below assume that you will be the person doing the testing with someone else, as I go into self muscle testing in the following section.

## Step by step

1. Your partner will stand facing you, slightly to the side, so that you are looking over each others' shoulders. You can also do this sitting down if you prefer (just ensure that the feet are flat on the ground and the legs are not crossed at the knees or ankles). The only requirement is that both you *and* your partner be sitting, or standing. It's important that the person who is doing the testing is not hovering over the person who is being tested. You need to be at roughly the same level.

2. Ask your partner to extend one arm (whichever they prefer) out to the side, parallel to the floor. Ask them to keep it stretched out.

3. Ask them to keep their chin parallel to the floor, eyes open, and facing down.

4. After getting permission from your partner, you will put your hand on their shoulder and on their wrist, and you will say "Be strong" or "resist" before gently pressing down on their wrist as they resist the pressure. Be sure to check with them to see if the pressure is at a good level. If you need to adjust, just play around until you find the best strength of pressure *for your partner.*

5. Test for a strong/weak response by checking true/false statements (things which your partner absolutely knows to be true). Ask them to say out loud: "My name is [Theirname]." This should test strong, meaning that their arm finds it easy to resist the pressure and remain parallel to the floor. Next, ask them to say out loud: "My name is [Nottheirname]." This should test weak, meaning that their arm will find it difficult to resist the pressure, and will be pushed downwards.

Be sure to use a name that doesn't correspond to anyone your partner actually knows, because this could generate a false positive. Try unusual names, or names that obviously don't correspond to your partner, such as names of celebrities. This may also get your partner laughing at the names you come up with, which will help them to relax into the process.

You can also use other statements that you and your partner absolutely know to be true/false, such as "The sun rises in the east" and "The sun rises in the west." "The sky is blue" (assuming you don't live in an area that suffers from extreme smog) and "The sky is orange."

6. Switch places and ask your partner to go through steps 1-5 with you, so you can experience muscle testing for yourself.

7. Now, you are ready to move onto the belief statements in this book, testing to see whether or not you (and your partner) hold the listed beliefs at the subconscious level.

There are other techniques for muscle testing with a partner. You can hold your arm out in front of you; you can hold your arm bent at your side in an L shape, and test only the forearm, or you can use a leg to muscle test. If the person is lying down, you can also have them raise their arm straight in the air, or bent at their side in an L shape. Search online for other examples of muscle testing with a partner if the examples above don't work easily, or if they have an injury.

* * *

## Self muscle testing

This is a bit tricky to explain in writing, which is why I've created a quick video that demonstrates each of these methods of self muscle testing. Many people find it tricky to get clear on which of these techniques is easiest for them. My best advice is to play around with them all until you find the best one for you (you may have noticed a theme here: finding what works for you as an individual is important in every step of this process).

## Finger circle

With one hand you make a circle with your finger and thumb, and with the other hand you insert one finger from the other hand into the circle and push the inside finger against the circle. You can use any finger, along with your thumb, to make the circle, and you can use any finger on your other hand to break the circle. Play around with it to see how much pressure it takes to force that circle to break or to hold, and then test it with the true and false questions.

Test: "My name is [Yourname]" and "My name is [Notyourname]" (or any of the examples above). When you try this method, it is also important to figure out which fingers are best for you to use during testing. When you make the circle, try your index finger, your middle finger, your ring finger, your pinkie; try all of your different fingers on both hands. The way I personally do it is to use my middle finger to make the circle with my thumb on my right hand, and I test with the index finger on my left hand (I'm left handed; for you it might be the other way around).

This is one of the most common ways that I use to do muscle testing on my own because I find it to be the easiest method for me . . . but again, this is all about finding the best method for *you*, which is why I've included six other methods for you to try.

## Fingers as arms

You can also use a method called fingers as arms (or maybe it's just me who calls it that), in which you place your hand flat on your leg, thigh or table, and raise up one finger to be the "arm" that you then press down on with a finger from your other hand.

Test: "My name is [Yourname]" and "My name is [Notyourname]" (or any of the examples above). As with the previous method, it is very important to figure out which fingers are best for you to use during testing. Try your index finger, your middle finger, your ring finger, your pinkie as the arm; try all of your different fingers on both hands. I personally find this method to be a bit difficult, but it works for some people, so give it a try.

## Double circles

This is very similar to the first technique, with the finger circle, except that in this method, you make two interlocking circles, which you then pull apart to test.

Test: "My name is [Yourname]" and "My name is [Notyourname]" (or any of the examples above). As with the previous methods, it is very important to figure out which fingers are best for you to use during testing. You can make the circles with different fingers.

## Sticky/smooth

In this method take, for example, your index finger and your thumb and rub them together as you test: "My name is [Yourname]," "My name is [Notyourname]." When you get the strong response it is very, very smooth when you are rubbing your fingers together and when you get the weak response it kind of "sticks" in the sense that it feels harder to rub your fingers together. Again, try different combinations of fingers to see what works for you: index and thumb, middle finger and thumb, ring finger and thumb, little finger and thumb.

This is another method that I find difficult because it's so subtle, but I've seen it work for people who struggle with some of the other methods.

## Scissors

In this method, you hold two fingers out, as if they were scissors, and then you press on them with two fingers from the other hand. You could even do your own version of the Vulcan greeting from Star Trek and make a larger scissors with two fingers on each side (that feels pretty awkward to me, but it's worth a try). Play around with different combinations of fingers and hands to see what's best for you. This is another one that I find a bit tricky, but give it a try and see if you like it.

## Stand and sway

This is another common technique. In stand and sway, you stand up, relax your knees, close your eyes and check for true and false. Say "My name is [Yourname]" and allow your body to be pulled either forward, backward, left, right, counter-clockwise, clockwise or not at all. And then give the weak or the false test: "My name is [Notyourname]," and then see how your body moves.

When I try this method, my strong is forward and my weak is backward. But it could be that your strong is left, and your weak is right. Your strong could be clockwise, your weak could be counter-clockwise; it is different for every person.

I find this method to be very easy, but also kind of a pain, as it involves standing up, which isn't always convenient when I'm doing a lot of work with myself. Also, it's pretty conspicuous, making it a bit awkward to use in public (unless you don't mind people staring and wondering what exactly you're doing).

## Pendulum

Another method that I use is a pendulum, and I've been using it for years. This is a method that a lot of people find to be easy to use, even those who struggle with the finger methods.

Test: "My name is [Yourname]" and "My name is [Notyourname]" (or any of the examples above). You can also say "Show me a yes" and "Show me a no." It might sway back and forth or side to side or clockwise or counter-clockwise. The response is different for every person. When I use the pendulum, the strong/yes response is forward and backward and the weak/no is from side to side, but (as in all of these methods) it may be different for you.

* * *

## Top mistakes

Here's a quick list of the top mistakes I see people making when using muscle testing. Use this list to troubleshoot whenever you encounter difficulties. Some people pick it up easily; others require time and practice to get it right.

## Improper position

No matter what technique you are using, you want to be sitting or standing with your chin parallel to the floor, and your eyes looking down. Your feet should be flat on the ground, and your legs should not be crossed at either the knees or the ankles. You should also be as relaxed as possible, while still sitting or standing up straight.

## No clear response

Whenever you start muscle testing, whether it's self muscle testing, or working with someone else, you always want to start out with the true/false test: "My name is [Yourname]", "My name is [Notyourname]". If you struggle to get a clear response with that, move onto other statements that you absolutely know to be true/false, such as "The sun rises in the east" and "The sun rises in the west." Also try "The sky is blue" (assuming you don't live in an area that suffers from extreme smog) and "The sky is orange."

Come up with other statements that you know to be true and false: "I am a human" and "I am a cat," for example. If you can make yourself laugh by coming up with silly statements to test, that will help you relax, which will then make the process easier.

## Not finding the right method

Another mistake that many people make is not finding the best method for them. Be sure to take the time to find what technique works for you. If you're struggling with self muscle testing, be sure you've exhausted all possibilities before giving up. Finally, get help if needed.

## Weak/weak response

One thing that can "go wrong" is when you get a weak/weak response. You might get a weak to your name and also a weak to the name that is not yours. In this situation, you might be dehydrated or you might need a snack. Have a drink of water, or have a bite of food if you think you're hungry, and test again. Keep drinking water (within reason—don't go overboard with it) until you test strong to the true statement and weak to the false statement.

## Strong/strong response

Sometimes you get a strong/strong response, which is when you get a strong to [Yourname] and also a strong to [Notyourname]. When this happens, you might simply need to calm down, relax, and get centered. You might be experiencing stress (particularly if you've been really struggling with muscle testing). If you've been experiencing problems with muscle testing for several minutes, take some time to rest and do something else before returning to your testing.

## Take action today

Watch my YouTube video that demonstrates each of these methods of self muscle testing, and test each one of them for yourself. Find which one works best for you.

If you have a friend or family member who is willing to experiment with you, try to muscle test with them. Invite them to try it with you so that you can see what it feels like.

## On the podcast

- 96 How To Use Muscle Testing In Your Business, with Holly Worton

# APPENDIX II

HOW TO USE THE BELIEF STATEMENTS

## Test your beliefs

You can use muscle testing, which you learned in the previous chapter, to see which of these beliefs you already hold at the subconscious level. This can be extremely useful, because often we think (at the conscious level) that we hold a particular belief, but in reality our subconscious is not on board with that belief. This means that we're stuck in a state of conflict, which keeps us stuck in  business.

Play around with the statements, and muscle test to see which beliefs you actually hold at the subconscious level and which ones you'll need to work on.

## Find the priority

Another way to use the list is to find which category of beliefs is the most important one to work on, and which are the priority belief statements to work on in each category. You can do this by using muscle testing to tap into your superconscious mind, or your higher self. That's the part of you that knows what's in your best interest and highest good, and when you set the intention, you can ask your higher self which areas are the highest priority for you to work on.

You can do this is by testing the following statement: *"The highest priority statement is in the category of Action & Goals."*

If that tests weak, then move onto the next category, and test: *"The highest priority statement is in the category of Change & Growth."*

Keep going until you find the right category. Once you've found the highest priority category, then ask which is the highest priority statement (for this example, I'm assuming a list of 35 statements): *"The highest priority statement is between numbers 1 and 18."*

If it tests strong, then narrow it down to the exact number. (*"The highest priority statement is between numbers 1 and 9." "Between 1 and 5." "Between 1 and 3." "The highest priority statement is number 1." "Number 2."*)

If it tests weak, test: *"The highest priority statement is between numbers 19 and 35."* Then, narrow down as in the above example.

Once you determine the highest priority statement, test to see if it's strong or weak. If weak, either work on changing the belief yourself (if you've done training in how to do so), or seek help from a trained professional who can work with you.

## Change your beliefs

If you've done training in a process or technique that works at the deeper levels, you can work with yourself to reprogram your beliefs. If you're new to changing beliefs at these deeper levels, you might want to either work with someone else or train in a technique that you feel drawn to. Find the best technique for you: Heart-centered Energy Work®, PSYCH-K®, ThetaHealing®, EFT (Emotional Freedom Technique), NLP (Neuro-Linguistic Programming), TAT (Tapas Acupressure Technique), hypnotherapy, or something else.

What I like about both PSYCH-K® and Heart-centered Energy Work® is that they are fast-acting, easy to use, forward-focused (they focuses on what you *do* want, not what you *don't* want), and they work with very specific beliefs and intentions. Also, as I've said before, Heart-centered Energy Work® functions by both reprogramming your subconscious beliefs *and* releasing energy blocks.

## Build a clear intention

You can also use the belief statements to help you build a clear intention of what you *do* want. The way I use Heart-centered Energy Work® is to build up a very clear vision and intention of what I actually want, and then I work on programming that intention into the subconscious, while at the same time releasing any energy blocks. If you're feeling stuck creating a clear vision of what you want for your business, read through the belief statements and select the most appropriate ones to build up your vision for your business.

Or you can spend some time journaling to get a clear vision of exactly what you want in your business: what your ideal work day looks like, how often you go on holiday, how much revenue you're bringing in, etc.

## APPENDIX III

NEED MORE HELP?

### Patreon

As I mentioned in the book, I've stepped back from doing one-to-one sessions so I can focus on my writing. However, I do offer occasional sessions in my Patreon community.

Head over to www.patreon.com/hollyworton and check it out. Please get in touch if you have any questions: holly@hollyworton.com.

### Podcast

The Into the Woods podcast is all about going into the woods of *you*. I've got plenty of episodes that discuss all areas of mindset and business beliefs. This is a great way to deepen your understanding of your own mindset, and find new ways of transforming your business beliefs. Most podcast episodes have full transcripts available on the website, either to read directly or as a free pdf download (no email required).

- 317 Holly Worton ~ Know Yourself: How to Answer the Question of "Where Am I Going?"
- 316 Holly Worton ~ Know Yourself: How to Answer the Question of "Where Am I?"
- 315 Holly Worton ~ Know Yourself: How to Answer the Question of "Who Am I?"
- 306 Holly Worton ~ How To Create New Habits That Last
- 297 Holly Worton ~ Personal Power: Why You Need It & How to Get It
- 295 Sharon Lock ~ How to Make Mindset Work a Habit
- 283 Joanna Hennon + Holly ~ Remember, It's Not Just About Energy:

Balancing the Inner and Outer Work

- 276 Holly Worton ~ How to Create Your Own Personal Formula For Mindset Work & Healing
- 272 Holly Worton ~ Mindset: Why It Isn't About Positive Thinking
- 270 Holly Worton ~ Why Mindset Matters
- 245 Holly Worton ~ How to Spring Clean Your Business + Mindset
- 230 Holly Worton ~ How to Make Mindset Work a Habit
- 221 Holly Worton ~ How Your Money Mindset Relates to Your Business Mindset
- 209 Carmen Spagnola ~ How Nature Can Get You The Right Mindset For Business
- 197 Holly Worton ~ Step into Your Greatness by Upgrading Your Business Beliefs
- 195 Holly Worton ~ How to Stay Grounded + Strong in Your Vision
- 192 Holly Worton ~ Get the Mindset You Need to Make a Big Impact
- 181 Jo Casey + Holly ~ Is Mindset Important in Business, or Is It Just an Excuse to Avoid Action?
- 170 Denise Duffield-Thomas ~ How Upgrading Your Money Mindset Can Transform Your Business
- 157 Holly Worton ~ How to Increase Your Visibility by Transforming Your Mindset
- 136 Holly Worton ~ Why You Can't Afford to Ignore Your Business Mindset
- 127 Holly Worton ~ How to Revolutionize Your Business Mindset for 2016
- 115 Holly Worton ~ How to Get the Right Mindset for Your Business
- 111 Holly Worton ~ How to Get Clear on Your Big Business Vision
- 96 How To Use Muscle Testing In Your Business, with Holly Worton

## One-to-one work

If you're ready to get started with one-to-one sessions right now, I have some recommendations for you. These are five women that I trust completely and often go to for sessions myself. They all work online via Skype/Zoom.

I highly recommend these five facilitators:

- Cara Wilde: http://carawilde.com
- Cazzie Dare: https://yearning4learning.co.uk/
- Claire Baker: http://happyhealthyempowered.com/
- Jo Trewartha: http://freeyourmindsolutions.com/
- Sharon Lock: http://sharonlock.com

# ABOUT THE AUTHOR

Holly Worton is a podcaster and nine times published author. Her latest book, *If Trees Could Talk: Life Lessons from the Wisdom of the Woods*, went straight to the top of 16 Amazon bestseller lists, and she has been featured on BBC Radio Scotland and on prime time national television in the UK – on ITV's This Morning.

She helps people get to know themselves better through connecting with Nature, so they can feel happier and more fulfilled. Holly enjoys spending time outdoors, walking long-distance trails and exploring Britain's sacred sites. She's originally from California and now lives in the Surrey Hills, but has also lived in Spain, Costa Rica, Mexico, Chile, and Argentina. Holly is a member of the Druid order OBOD.

Holly ran her first business for ten years, building it up to become a multi-million-dollar enterprise. When she went into the coaching world she was confident that she had the business and marketing skills she needed to set up a new company. And she did – but she struggled to grow her new venture quickly because she encountered fears, blocks, and limiting beliefs that she didn't even know she had.

She discovered that pushing forward and taking action just wasn't enough. She needed to transform her mindset and release her blocks, as this was the only way to take the *right* actions to move her new business forward. Thus began her journey of intense personal development through deep mindset work, which transformed her existing coaching business into a focus on helping people with their business mindset.

Eventually, she realized that she wanted to devote her time to helping people through her writing, and she let go of her mindset business to focus on her books. Now, Holly continues to write about mindset, long-distance walking, and connecting to Nature.

## Podcast

You can find her podcast on Apple Podcasts, or wherever you listen to podcasts. Links to subscribe, as well as the full list of episodes, can be found here: http://www.hollyworton.com/podcast/.

## Patreon

You can join her online community where you can receive the benefits of her done-for-you mindset work, and also get discounts on one-to-one sessions, by joining her on Patreon: https://www.patreon.com/hollyworton.

## Books

You can find her other books, including her books on nature, walking long-distance trails and business mindset, wherever you purchased this book.

## Newsletter

Finally, you can stay in touch by subscribing to her newsletter on her main website: http://www.hollyworton.com/.

# Also by Holly Worton

## Business books

- *Business Beliefs: Upgrade Your Mindset to Overcome Self Sabotage, Achieve Your Goals, and Transform Your Business (and Life)*
- *Business Blocks: Transform Your Self-Sabotaging Mind Gremlins, Awaken Your Inner Mentor, and Allow Your Business Brilliance to Shine*
- *Business Blocks: A Companion Workbook*
- *Business Intuition: Tools to Help You Trust Your Own Instincts, Connect with Your Inner Compass, and Easily Make the Right Decisions*
- *Business Intuition: A Companion Workbook*
- *Business Visibility: Mindset Shifts to Help You Stop Playing Small, Dimming Your Light and Devaluing Your Magic*
- *Business Visibility: A Companion Workbook*

## Nature books

- *If Trees Could Talk: Life Lessons from the Wisdom of the Woods*
- *If Trees Could Talk: Life Lessons from the Wisdom of the Woods — A Companion Workbook*

## Walking books

- *Alone on the South Downs Way: One Woman's Solo Journey from Winchester to Eastbourne*
- *Walking the Downs Link: Planning Guide & Reflections on Walking from St. Martha's Hill to Shoreham-by-Sea*
- *Alone on the Ridgeway: One Woman's Solo Journey from Avebury to Ivinghoe Beacon*
- *Walking the Wey-South Path: Planning Guide & Reflections on Walking from Guildford to Amberley*

# A Request

If you enjoyed this book, please review it online. It takes just a couple of minutes to write a quick review. It would mean the world to me! Good reviews help other readers to discover new books.

Thank you, thank you, thank you.

Made in United States
North Haven, CT
09 October 2022